Making A's in College

What Top College Students Know About Getting Straight A's

The Study-Professor's Guide

Sandra U. Gibson, Ph.D.
James R. Gibson, Jr. M.A.

Workbooks Press
Atlanta, GA

Making A's in College

Electronic editions published 2011, 2013, 2014, 2017, 2018 by Workbooks Press, a division of Hickory Cove Music, Atlanta, GA.

Completely revised and updated, 2017. First print edition 2019.

ISBN: 9781797049830

yourcollegesuccess@gmail.com

Disclaimer
The study techniques and strategies described in this book come from many years of working with college and high-school students and are helpful for most students. However it is not possible to make guarantees about specific results, and we make no claim that any individual reader of this book will achieve at a high level.

If a student has serious learning or attention problems, it is important and useful to seek professional help. Many colleges have counseling centers which offer a range of benefits to students with learning, and other, issues.

If you have problems with depression or emotional problems you should seek professional help. Start with the counseling center at your school, but be sure to get the help you need to get the most from your college years.

TABLE OF CONTENTS

A Message From Dr. Gibson

Welcome to the *Making A's in College* system for building high performance and getting good grades in college. My goal is to show you how to study more efficiently so you'll learn more in less time.

During your school years you've learned a lot about many specific subjects.

Unfortunately, if you're like many students, you haven't been taught *how to learn.* That's too bad, because it's a crucial skill, and it's one you'll need for the rest of your life.

As you know, we live in the information age. Available knowledge now doubles so quickly that even the experts no longer know how much information is out there, but it's increasing very, very fast.

And, since so much of this information flood is *instantly accessible,* it's easy to be overwhelmed.

In fact, today's students face a new, difficult, set of problems: *how do you cope with all this always-available information*?

How do you even find the time to read it?

How can you decide what's important?

Will you be able to remember it once you locate the information you need in the mass of data that's out there?

Stop and think about this fascinating fact: one daily issue of *The New York Times* (which you may read on your phone) contains *more* information than the average person living in the 16th century would encounter *in an entire lifetime.*

Isn't that astounding? One issue of a daily paper, which is instantly accessible, contains more information than most people in Shakespeare's time would encounter in their lives!

So, we're living in a time when we are flooded—constantly overwhelmed—with a tsunami of information. And you're entering college where *you'll have more and more information thrown at you every single day.*

Thus, learning *how* to learn is, honestly, a survival skill.

When you use the techniques from this book, you'll know how to learn effectively, and you'll develop useful habits for managing all that new information.

In over 25 years at Georgia State University, a large university in the center of Atlanta, I've taught thousands of college and university students in seminars, classes, and workshops.

And I've worked with hundreds of individuals, from mothers returning to college to surgeons preparing for certification exams. I've done workshops for high-school and even middle-school students, and I raised two children who had successful college careers.

I've spent a LOT of time working with study skills in many different contexts, and I have learned what works and what's important.

The strategies I teach in seminars, workshops, classes, and in this book, work well for two reasons.

First, these methods take advantage of the way your brain *actually works*. They are based on years of scientific study and careful experiments.

And second, when you use the learning techniques in this book, you'll be *active.* You won't be daydreaming or lost in space. Your mind will be in gear, focused on the task at hand. *I strongly believe that active learning is the best way to learn.*

So, throughout this book you'll find **Personal Learning System Action Steps**, called *PLS Action Steps*.

Since *active learning* is the very foundation of this book, I hope you'll actually do the *PLS* steps, try them out, and then make them part of your own learning style. When you do, these approaches and techniques will become automatic, and you'll be learning effectively and efficiently.

I wish you good luck on your exciting lifelong adventure with learning . . . and I hope your GPA will be a 4.0!

Sandra U. Gibson, Ph.D.
Atlanta, GA

PART ONE: GET STARTED

Why Good Grades Are Really Important

Get the Most from *Making A's in College*

Develop Your *Personal Learning System*

Multitasking is NOT Your Friend

Deal With Digital Distraction

Chapter 1

Why Good Grades Are Really Important

In a word, good grades are important in college because they can open doors for you.

There are lots of other reasons that you would want good grades, but perhaps the main one is that *you need to be prepared for whatever direction your future may take.*

And you don't really know, usually, what that will be—there are likely to be surprises and unforeseen twists and turns in your life. That's completely normal—no one can really see the future.

So it's only sensible to do what you can to keep all those future options open.

To illustrate this point, here's an example from our own family. When our son went to college, he was planning to be a history teacher. In fact, he did graduate from a large state university with a degree in history.

But, surprisingly, about half-way through college he decided that he really wanted to go to medical school. Fortunately, his grades from the first two years of college were very good, and he was able to get into a fine medical school. Now he's a doctor.

When he entered college, *no one* could possibly have guessed that medical school was in his future. Had our son's grades been poor, or even marginal, during the first two years, it would have been very difficult (or even impossible) for him to be admitted to a top med school.

The truth is that, in most cases, you just don't know what you'll want to do in two years, five years, or later in your life. *Good grades will keep your options open.*

Practical Reasons Good Grades Matter

Of course, keeping future options open isn't the only reason to keep your grades up. There are more immediate, very practical reasons, too.

1. At the most basic level, *you need to stay in school.* Poor grades are a quick way to get kicked out of college. Yes, you may be young, and naturally you're excited by new friends and freedoms, but being on academic probation or exclusion because of poor grades is really a poor career move.

2. If you've been awarded a scholarship, you doubtlessly must maintain a certain GPA *to continue to get funding.* When you look at it this way, your study time could be easily translated into dollars-per-hour. Scholarships are, in a way, paying you to do well.

In fact, while you are in school, it can be very useful to *think of college as your job.*

3. Honor societies, the Dean's List, and other kinds of recognition come to students who make good grades. Such honors look good on your resume, of course, but there is another immediate benefit: *you*

are in the company of other high-achieving students, and you'll benefit in lots of ways from contact with bright, motivated people.

In fact, contact with bright, motivated fellow-students can be one of the best things you'll get from college. You'll learn more from these fellow students, have fun doing it, and you'll likely make friends for life—friends who share your interests.

4. On a personal level, *it feels good to reach a goal* and to achieve. Good grades are one measure of your accomplishments and give you a very good (and real) reason to feel great about yourself and what you've attained.

One More Reason

It's true that you can learn a lot without worrying about grades, and sometimes you may resent the time spent preparing for tests and writing papers. Students often feel that working for good grades actually interferes with real learning, and it's true that they aren't the same thing.

But there is a lot of value in completing long tasks and showing that you can follow through with continuing projects such as research papers, classes, and successful semesters.

It's certainly possible that your future employer won't care what you know about geology, or geometry, or geography. But good grades in those classes show that you know how to complete important assignments and that you finish projects on time.

These are important skills, and good grades show mastery of them just as much as mastery of specific subject matter.

It's going to be very tempting to stay in bed some cold morning rather than go to an early class or to just do the minimal amount to slide by on a paper, but if you can keep the larger picture in mind, you'll benefit greatly in the long run.

Chapter 2

Get the Most from *Making A's in College*

This is a how-to book, a handbook, really, on how to go do college and it includes lots of tips, suggestions, strategies, and ideas designed to help you learn more effectively. Some of the ideas may be new to you, and we'll get started by using one of the reading techniques that will be covered in more detail later.

There's no need to wait—let's plunge right in so that you'll learn more from *this* book as you read it!

It doesn't matter whether you're reading a traditional paper book, or on your computer or a Kindle—the approach to learning effectively while you read is exactly the same.

One of the very important (and often overlooked) reading skills you'll learn later is the surprising value of spending a bit of time *previewing* what you're about to tackle.

Previewing gives you a mini-roadmap of what you're going to learn, and it prepares your mind for efficient learning.

So, now let's *preview* this book and look at how to get the most from it in the shortest time.

A Thumbnail Preview

Here is a thumbnail description of what you'll learn as you read this book and an outline of how it's organized.

The book begins with a section called *Get Started*, which includes discussions about why grades are important, setting up your own approach to studying smarter, and ideas for controlling digital distraction.

Then, since much of your college success is based on non-scholastic skills, the next section of this book is called *Support Skills*.

These are vital to your success and include overcoming procrastination, getting organized, managing your time, building concentration, and an important (but short) explanation of *how our memory actually works*.

Part three of this book, the core, is devoted to the *Academic Skills* you'll need in college. They include note-taking, the **PART** reading system, active studying, building your memory, being testwise, and managing test anxiety.

The final section is called *Bonus Tips for College Success*, and presents 21 more practical smart-study ideas, interviews with seven successful students who describe what study strategy they find most useful, and a review page that summarizes "Eleven Commandments for College Success."

That's a quick overview, a small roadmap of where you'll be going in the book and what you'll be learning. It's a logical arrangement, designed to quickly give you proven skills that you can immediately use to make better grades.

How to Use This Book

Making A's in College presents dozens of different tips, techniques, methods, ideas and strategies for doing well in college. That's a lot of new information and you won't master it all at once.

So, think of this book as a continuing resource, like an exercise program for your mind. Come back to it when you have a problem with a particular issue—note-taking, reading, or test anxiety, for example—and review the tips and suggestions.

Remember, this book comes from many years of helping students succeed in college. These techniques work, but you won't try to use them all at once.

In fact, you probably won't need them all—you may be very organized, but need help with test anxiety, while another student may breeze through tests, but have trouble keeping up with assignments. So use the ideas that you think will benefit *you*.

Be sure your mind is in gear and that you are ready to concentrate as you read because there's little point in reading this, or any, book when you're distracted, tired, or preoccupied with another activity.

In fact, *studying while distracted* is often worse than pointless. Later, we'll discuss lots of ways to build strong concentration, but for now, as you read this book be sure that you are *focused* and paying attention to what you read.

Don't make just one pass. Some of the techniques taught here—the reading and note-taking systems, for example—may take some time to master. You'll probably need to read a chapter in this book, think about it, try it, and come later back to re-read the chapter.

You'll find that in building strong study skills (as in many things), *practice makes perfect.*

Just Do It!

Finally, to get the most from this book, be sure to really do the *Personal Learning System (PLS) Action Steps*.

Simply reading about them won't work, and just thinking about the steps isn't very effective.

These action steps are designed so you can make the best use of all the strategies and techniques in this book by helping you focus on what *you* need. The steps are hands-on practice of what you're learning, and they'll illustrate the value of these new ideas.

Then, use the new techniques from this book regularly as you study. You may already be a good student who uses many of these study methods, or you may not have done well in school.

Perhaps you're returning after many years out of school. In all these situations, you'll benefit from making *good study techniques* into *good study habits*.

Once you see how effective the tips and techniques here can be, you'll understand that turning them into your standard operating procedure will be of great benefit!

Chapter 3

Develop YOUR Personal Learning System

Different people learn in different ways. That's why it's important to develop your own *Personal Learning System.*

The study techniques that work best for you may not help another student, so your study system will reflect *your own* strengths and preferences. It will also pinpoint areas that need work. That's why we call it the 'PERSONAL Learning System.'

With the *Personal Learning System* (PLS) activities at the end of each chapter, you'll answer such questions as:

When is the best time for me to study?

Where is the best place for me to study?

What kinds of *distractions* are the biggest problems for me?

What *memory-building* techniques work best for me?

Which *study strategies* help me the most?

What approaches help me *do best on tests*?

How can I improve my *note-taking*?

How can I apply the **PART** reading system?

What steps can I take to manage *test anxiety*?

What is my best technique for managing *digital distraction*?

Here's how to create your own *Personal Learning System* profile. It's not a lot of trouble, and it won't take much time, but it will help you get the most from the *Making A's in College* study system.

After all, you're going to spend thousands of hours in college, and tens of thousands of dollars paying for it—so it makes a lot of sense to spend a few hours making sure you are ready.

The *PLS Action Steps* will really help you focus on what YOU need and they'll help you put into action the ideas you've just learned.

Six Action Steps for You

So, throughout this book there are 17 *PLS Action Steps* to help you apply new learning techniques to your own study life. To use them most effectively:

1. Get a notebook to use for your *PLS* system or, if you like, simply use a section of your binder.

Of course you can just make a folder on your computer for this purpose, but often it's simpler and quicker to just use old-fashioned pen and paper.

2. Be sure you actually *write* the *PLS* steps. *Writing* is a big step toward *active learning.*

And throughout this book, ACTIVE LEARNING is our goal.

Simply thinking about these mini-assignments, or just reading about them, won't do you nearly as much good as writing them down.

3. As you go through this book, follow the instructions for each *PLS Action Step*. They aren't difficult or time-consuming, but they will focus your attention on how to apply new skills *to your own situation*.

Some are surprisingly simple, but they can revolutionize your study habits. I've seen it happen time after time.

4. Many of the *PLS* steps ask you to make lists. Use brainstorming techniques to make these lists as long and complete as possible. That is, think of as many points as you can and *write them down*.

As you probably know, brainstorming works best when you freely come up with lots of ideas without worrying about their practicality or relevance. The important first step is to think about the problem or solution and make a long list of your ideas.

Remember that your *Personal Learning System* is for you alone to see, so be honest and complete as you think about your study habits and problems, your own weaknesses and strengths.

5. When you discover a new study method that works well for you, put it into use as soon as possible. Some of the learning techniques in this book will take practice at first, but before long you'll be using them automatically, and you'll be learning more effectively than ever.

6. However, don't expect to use *all* the study methods in you'll read here. Select the ones that *you* need, the ones that may help you the most.

Many students who attend my seminars and workshops tell me that just one idea is enough to change C's to A's. I've heard this over and over, and have often seen how just one idea can revolutionize a student's academic life. (And it's often a very simple tip that makes the difference.)

Refer to your *PLS* notebook when you need a boost in study power or when you're facing a difficult study situation. It will remind you of what works best for you.

Be patient. Don't expect instant results. Even with these new study techniques, most students won't change overnight from a 2.5 to a 3.8 GPA. New habits take time to establish, and old ones can be very hard to break.

But the important thing is to start working on improving your grades in a methodical way.

You'll be in college for a long time, so it's worthwhile to make an effort to find the best ways for *you* to learn, and to get in the habit of using them. That's what the *Personal Learning System* is for. We hope you'll use it!

To Repeat . . . Just Do It!

But, I can hear you asking, "Do I really need to DO these *PLS Action Steps*? Isn't it enough just to read them over?"

Here's why it matters whether you *do* the steps. There is a great difference in reading about something and actually doing it.

Reading about tennis is vastly different from *playing* the game. Watching a video about how to play the guitar won't turn you into a musician. You have to practice. There's not a shortcut.

With most subjects, you learn best by doing, and that's why the **Personal Learning System Action Steps** are so important. They're simple, but they *focus your attention on how specific study skills can help you.* By taking a few minutes to DO the activity, you are actively learning it. It's a simple technique, but it works.

So just do it!

PLS Action Step 1

On the first page of your *PLS* notebook, list any study problems you have. Be specific as you analyze your current strengths and weaknesses.

Do you procrastinate? Have trouble concentrating?

Need improvement in your reading skills? Wonder how to take good notes in class?

Write "My Study Problems" at the top of the page and list all the difficulties you can think of. No one else needs to see this list. It's for you alone to use, so be honest as you diagnose where you are right now.

As you go through the rest of this book, watch for ideas that can help you solve the specific problems you've identified in this first *PLS* Action Step.

You may not need all the skills we discuss, and that's why this *self-assessment* list is a great starting place for improving *your* study skills.

It's focused on *your* current situation, and will help you make specific, targeted improvements that will benefit *you.*

So, think about YOUR study problems and your own situation. Make a list of the problems. We'll spend the rest of the book working on solving them.

Chapter 4

Multitasking is NOT Your Friend: Deal With Digital Distraction

You might think that you can be more effective and save time by doing several things at once.

But you'd be mistaken.

We live in a world that operates at hyper-speed most of the time, and we're bombarded by so much information, we have so much to do, and are pulled in so many different directions that we often try to save a little time by doing two (or more) things at once. It becomes first a habit and then an addiction.

Just look around. People are texting at almost every stoplight (despite the well-known dangers and the fact that it's illegal). Students in the library are often paying more attention to their cellphones than to the book that's open in front of them.

Multitasking is everywhere. Its the normal state of affairs for most people.

If you're reading this book, it's likely that you've been surrounded by personal electronics and social media all your life. It's clearly the norm.

But when you're in college, it will pay you to ask: *is all this multitasking helping me?*

Or hurting me?

Is it making it easier and quicker for me to learn ? Or harder?

Sure, you can listen to music while you wash the dishes. You can talk to your passengers while you drive a car. You can walk and chew gum at the same time, so there are some things that *can* be combined.

But as you probably know from many recent news stories, research shows what common sense also tells us—you can't text and do anything else at the same time. Most of these stories focus, of course, on texting and driving, which is now illegal in most states for demonstrated safety reasons.

But isn't driving different from schoolwork? Can't you study and do other things at the same time? Like watch TV, check your phone, text your friends, and post on Instagram? Is that really so bad?

Here's what Dr. Marcel Just, a neuroscientist at Carnegie Mellon University says about multitasking. "There's only so much brain capability at any one time, you might call it 'throughput.' You can divide it down as much as you want to, but the price will be even higher, then.

"Multitasking with no cost is a myth. There's no free lunch . . ." (from PBS *Newshour*, January 5, 2011). Clearly this is not recent news—it's been studied and known for years.

Let's repeat that point for emphasis: *Multitasking with no cost is a myth. There's no free lunch.*

This is born out by study after study. For example, current research shows that trying to send text or email messages while you're driving is *at least as dangerous as driving drunk.*

It turns out that when concentration is involved, the human brain does not have multiple channels. It's not a dual- or quad-core processor like your computer, or even your phone.

The brain works best when it focuses on ONE task at a time.

These findings have very important implications for your college life as studies continue to show the futility, inefficacy, or even danger, from multitasking.

Hyperspeed is the New Normal

Think how life and electronics have changed just in the past few years. You carry a smartphone and probably a laptop with you. You may also have an iPad or Android tablet in your backpack.

You probably have a Facebook, Instagram, Twitter, YouTube, Tumblr, Vine, Snap and many more social network options. You may be reading this book on a Kindle or other ebook reader.

You are thus under constant temptation to check email, update Facebook, tweet your friends with your latest thoughts or whereabouts and on and on and on.

In a major *New York Times* series of articles on digital distraction, (*The New York Times*, 11/21/2010) a particularly honest student said, "I know I *can* read a book, but then I'm up and checking Facebook. Facebook is amazing because it feels like you're doing something but you're not really doing anything. It's the absence of doing something, but you feel gratified anyway."

That's a pretty tough and honest view of how social media can waste enormous amounts of time.

And of course it's not just Facebook—the same thing is true for other social networks. They are interesting, immediate, stimulating, and fun, but very tempting time-traps that can steal hours from your day.

Here's the real bottom line: television, DVDs, games, and even constant music are also intrusive if you're trying to do something that requires concentration.

Learning Requires Concentration

Studying requires concentration. *If you aren't paying attention while you are studying, you are wasting your time.*

You'll read, in chapter 17, that two of the successful students we interviewed said that they even find music to be distracting when they are seriously studying.

College really is your job now, and you are your own CEO. Here's an interesting thing to do if you're interested in how top executives think about distraction and productivity. Simply do a YouTube search for "Productivity" and you'll find many top (and highly paid) trainers teaching executives how to be more productive.

Interestingly, many of the techniques taught to business leaders are the same as those taught in this book, because executives and students face similar challenges.

Often, an executive trainers' message is the same as the message in this chapter: if you want to improve your productivity, you MUST focus.

In fact, many top trainers teach their clients to simply TURN OFF email, texting, Instagram, and Facebook for periods during the day when they need to work on important projects. (And in college, there are lots of important projects.)

If this strategy for combating distraction works for top executives, and if it's important for them—it will work for you, too.

But isn't this difficult to do?

Yes, it can be very, very hard. We all like our digital gadgets, we all like being connected, and the appeal of such constant connection can be literally addictive.

But ask yourself these questions:

Do I really have time to waste?

Do I have extra time?

Who is in control of my time, anyway?

Here's the bottom-line question: *Can you afford to cheat yourself out of part of the education you're paying and working for?*

Overcoming digital distraction is a hard thing to do, but it's really worthwhile. It's ultimately proving to yourself that YOU, and not electronic gadgets, are in control of your life. It's proving to yourself that YOU and not manipulative engineers in Silicon Valley are in charge of YOUR own life.

Digital Distraction vs. Being There

You've probably heard the phrase, "be in the moment." It means *to be present*, to give your full attention to whatever you are doing.

This isn't rocket science, but it can be very hard to do—and it is really important.

Thus, you're a better driver if you give your FULL attention to driving.

Your personal relationships will be better if you give your FULL attention to your friends and family while you are with them.

And your college life will be much, much more successful if you don't try to split your attention into pieces.

So, if you need to check your email, then by all means check your email. Update Facebook if you'd like to as well.

But don't constantly do these things while you are studying. Your brain can't really handle it and you'll end up short-changing yourself.

And, if you're studying, or reading a chapter and you zip over to Instagram or Vine for a minute, you know exactly what will happen. One thing will lead to another, and you'll suddenly have spent (or wasted) ten, twenty, thirty minutes.

Or more.

Plus, it will take you time to get your focus back to studying. It's far better, and far more efficient, to set aside time for checking social media, and LIMIT that time while your goal is study.

The same thing goes for watching TV, movies, and YouTube while you are studying. *Neither you, I, nor anyone else can read, think, write, or study at top efficiency while being distracted by a movie.*

We'll talk more about the best place and time for you to study later in this book, but for now, realize that when you are reading, *put aside distractions and read.*

And when you are working on math problems, *put aside*

distractions and do the math. FOCUS makes a huge difference.

When you are studying, that is, it only makes sense to put aside distractions and study. The distractions will still be there when you've finished your work, and you'll feel better because you didn't cheat your study time.

(Digital distraction is now widely recognized as a major problem in contemporary society, and lots of different approaches are emerging to fight it. One of the most drastic are "digital free" camps and retreats for adults that help people regain balance and focus and take control of their own lives again.)

Don't Be Distracted in Class

College isn't cheap. In fact, for most students and their families it's a huge expense. Your parents may be making a big sacrifice to send you to school, and you may be working a part-time (or even full-time) job to help pay your way.

You or your family may be going into significant debt so you can go to college. Even if you're on a scholarship, *someone* is paying for your education.

Your professors want you to be engaged in what's happening in class. After all, isn't that why you are in college in the first place?

But if you are fooling with your digital devices, it's obvious to the teacher that you aren't paying attention. And professors don't like that at all.

There are several videos on YouTube of a professor pouring liquid nitrogen over a laptop in front of a stunned class to illustrate his extremely low opinion of distraction during class time.

Even if the laptop was just an old one sacrificed to make a point, the teacher's anger is clear and very real. It's a good point to remember.

Colleges have tried different approaches to this problem, from turning off internet access (as the University of Chicago Law School did) to simply banning laptops from the classroom.

Is avoiding distraction in class really that important? Yes, if you're interested in making good grades.

So, if you fool with your phone, send texts during class, or surf the web while a professor is speaking, you're probably irritating your teacher (who has a clear view of what you're doing).

Who Suffers When You're Distracted in Class?

OK, your professor is probably aggravated when students ignore the lecture to fool with digital devices. But who is it really hurting?

In fact, a study at the University of Colorado at Boulder found that students who fiddle with their laptops during class scored 11 percent lower on exams than students who paid attention.

Distraction in class may *aggravate* your instructor—but it's *hurting* YOU.

After all, you are paying tuition to be there, and if you aren't paying attention, you're wasting a lot of money.

Do you have money to waste? Did you or your parents borrow college money just to fritter it away? Of course not!

A Real Example With Bad Results

We know a college student who works in the graduate admissions office of a major university. Part of her job is to take prospective MBA students to sit in on classes so they can see this competitive graduate program first-hand.

One of the bright prospective students she took to visit a graduate business class spent most of his visiting time emailing and texting from his phone. And he—the prospective students—was sitting in clear view of the professor. He even took a selfie during the lecture.

The admissions guide was concerned, but she didn't intervene, She decided, correctly, that the prospective student should be himself on this visit so the professors could assess him while he was looking at the MBA program.

In this case, fooling with his phone kept the prospect out of this excellent MBA program. Immediately after class, the professor called the admissions office and said, "I want that prospective student's file flagged. He's NOT to be admitted to this program. We don't want students who won't pay attention and aren't interested." This student may never know why he wasn't admitted to this nationally-ranked MBA program, but now you know.

And you can learn from his mistake.

(When we checked on this story to verify it, we found that this was not the only time that a visiting prospective student had been marked for exclusion because of digital distraction during a class visit.

An admissions official told us that it's one of the guidelines used in evaluating possible students, and that professors commonly add "Do Not Admit" to student files when they observe such behavior.)

This is really common sense, isn't it? You know that you can't text and drive safely, and you know that it's rude to ignore your dinner companion and talk endlessly on a cellphone.

The key point here is *that texting, web surfing, and emailing in class and during your study time is counterproductive.*

Or worse.

PLS Action Step 2

Think about whether digital distraction is a problem for you, as it is for most students.

It will be helpful to keep a log for a few days of your "digital time" so you can see how much time you actually spend online and with your digital devices. It will give you a clear idea of what you might need to do to get control of these habits.

Use a small pocket notebook or even a piece of paper in your pocket. Make several columns, one for each electronic device or habit you have. You could have a column, then, for TV, YouTube, Facebook, Instagram, Snap, Twitter, your phone, iPad, online games, email, and so on.

Then, jot down approximately how much time you spend when you check your Facebook page, or surf the web, watch TV, and enjoy YouTube or Vine. Include other apps, programs, sites, and devices you visit frequently.

This is a time to really be honest with yourself, because digital distraction is a huge problem in college (as it is in the workplace).

If you are to control your own time, you need to have a clear idea of where that time is going.

So, for three or four typical days, keep a careful record and then total up the time you've spent connected to your electronics.

That way, when we talk about time management in chapter seven, you'll already have this important information to use as you work on effective ways to be in control your most valuable resource—your time.

PART TWO: SUPPORT SKILLS

Overcome Procrastination—How to *Really* Get Started

Get It Together—How to Organize All That Work

Time Marches On—But You Can Manage It

How to Build Your Concentration

How Your Memory Works (and Why It
Sometimes Doesn't)

Chapter 5

Overcome Procrastination—How to *Really* Get Started

If you're like most students, you sometimes have trouble getting started on assignments and projects. You hope to get everything done, but you think, "Not right now. I'll do it later."

Maybe you're just not interested in the subject so you don't work on the assignments.

Maybe you have so much to do and so many big projects that you're overwhelmed.

And maybe your social life is claiming a lot (or even most) of your time.

Or maybe you need to work on a big project, and you just don't know where to begin. So you put it off.

But research papers, reading assignments, and exams won't go away.

Even worse, if you put them off, problems increase because *you'll have even more to do tomorrow*. That is, tomorrow, you'll have *tomorrow's* work to do, plus *today's.*

And maybe yesterday's isn't quite finished either.

Start a Project to Overcome Inertia

If you've ever had a physics class, then you know about inertia. A body at rest requires a certain amount of energy to move it—otherwise it will just remain where it is.

Or, if you've ever pushed a car with a dead battery, you know that it takes more energy to just get the car moving on the street than it does to keep it rolling.

It's often the *first effort* that's hard, but it's making that first effort that will move you from just thinking about a class project to actually DOING it.

If you tend to procrastinate, or have a hard time getting started, then it's important for you to do *something*—even if it's something small—to get the project in motion. And that's where setting realistic goals, breaking down projects into small bits, and using to-do lists, are useful strategies to know and use.

If you have trouble getting to work on assignments and big projects, these three approaches will help.

First, Set a Goal

First, set a realistic, reachable goal for each project. Don't make it a huge, grand-sounding goal or you'll probably give up in frustration. Instead, *break your goals down so you can reach part of them each day.*

For example, saying to yourself, "My goal is to make all A's this semester," is an excellent long-range goal. *But, to reach it you need to set daily goals.* For example, you might break it down this way, and say:

"My goal is to make an A in this class, so here's exactly what I will do to make it happen.

"I'm going to make an A on each paper I hand in.

"I'm going to be prepared for each class, and I'll participate in discussions.

"I'm going to study and aim for an A on each test I take this semester.

"That means I have to study *every day* to keep up with assignments."

That's the way to make goals work for you. Break larger goals down into smaller, do-able bits, and accomplish them one by one. It's a strategy to keep a big project from seeming overwhelming.

And by breaking projects down into smaller pieces, you can more easily create a road-map to getting it all done.

Here's an example. Let's assume that you have a project for your marketing class to create a presentation about how an American company changes its marketing approach in different cultures. This sounds like a big project, and it is, but it will help you to think about the project's individual components so you can see exactly what you need to do.

How to Break It Down

To get started on a big project like this, then, the first step is to think about what you have to do, and *break it down into manageable tasks*. Here's how you might go about it:

34

1. What company will I choose? Maybe I'll choose McDonald's because I think I know something about how they market in the U.S. It should be easy to find information on their marketing, since it's such a huge multinational company. There are probably even books about it, and that would be easy to research.

2. What other culture will I use for this project? I think I'll research McDonald's in France because I like France, and I know the French have immense respect for food. First thing to do is to see if there is a website for McDonald's French division.

3. Then I need to research McDonald's marketing approach in France, so I'll search online, at the company website, and in broad Google searches, and I'll look in marketing resources in the library.

4. I'll talk to my professor after class about my idea and see if she has any suggestions for relevant sources.

5. Once I begin to accumulate some data, I'll have a better idea for whether this should be a PowerPoint presentation or just a report. Then I'll create a timeline for pulling all this information together into a good presentation.

You still don't have any information about your project because you haven't done any research yet, but you have broken the vague idea of a class presentation down into five specific tasks, and you'll do them one at a time.

Each item you've listed above gives you a direction, a sense of where you need to go.

So now you have constructed a set of good, manageable goals.

Now, they don't seem overwhelming.

Now they even seem like something you could—*and will*—do.

So, here's the first step to overcome procrastination: *set goals you can reach one step at a time.*

Don't even try to do everything at once, because that's counter-productive and frustrating.

And when you've read chapter seven, on time management, you'll understand how useful it is to plan backward on big projects by making a *timeline* so you can manage the project's tasks in a stress-free way.

Here's a simple motto that's useful as you go through college. We heard it first from a football coach, but it applies to your studies, too.

By the yard it's hard.
By the inch, it's a cinch!

Yes, you do have a lot of work to do and there's much more to come before you graduate. But when you tackle projects *one step at a time*, then one class at a time, then one semester at a time, you'll be on your way.

Another Example

Here's another example of how to break down a big project. Let's say a major assignment in English class this term is to write a fifteen-page research paper on how Charles Dickens' life is reflected in the novel *David Copperfield.*

That's a big assignment. How do you get started?

First, organize this task by making a list of what you have to do. Such a list might look like this:

1. Get a copy of *David Copperfield* and a biography of Charles Dickens.

2. Read both books.

3. Take notes on each book.

4. Do research online and in the library, if needed, to gather more information.

5. Outline ideas for this paper.

6. Save all digital files in two places.

7. Write a rough first draft.

8. Revise the draft, making corrections and changes.

9. Let the paper sit for a day or two.

10. Re-read, revise, and correct.

11. Print the final version.

12. Turn in an excellent paper, on time.

Now, even though you have all term to work on this project, *it is very important not to wait until the last minute to get started.*

You already know what will happen if you wait: stress, rushing to finish, a poor paper, and a poor grade (which will result in more stress).

Use a "To-Do List" to Manage a Big Project

Use the to-do list (described below) and your calendar to break tasks such as this one down into do-able parts. Write these tasks on your list. You'll find it much easier to start and finish assignments *when you break a big project down into manageable parts.*

Once you've done that, start with goal number one.

And here's a helpful hint: if you really have a tendency to procrastinate, make step number one *very* easy, as in the example below. The important thing is to actually *get started* on the project.

Make a start by *overcoming inertia, even if it's a small, easy step.* Then, you'll be moving forward!

To stay with the example above, let's see how you might follow those steps:

1. Check out *David Copperfield* and a biography of Dickens from the library *today.*

(If you couldn't find the book in the library, stop by the bookstore, check online booksellers, or just download an ebook version. Your Kindle will make this task very easy and quick.)

Don't let this step be a bottleneck. Locating the books you need can be problematic if you're in a rush and other students need the same thing. And while millions of books are available as ebooks, some aren't, especially scholarly or small-press books that are more obscure.

(Note: in this example, David Copperfield is an old work, so it's in the *public domain*—that is, the book is no longer protected by copyright. Such books are almost always free, or very inexpensive, in digital editions and they often include lots of extra critical or historical information.)

2. Read the novel. Divide the number of pages by the time you have to set a daily reading goal.

3. Now, read the biography, breaking it down into daily chunks as you did with the novel.

4. Finish reading both the biography and the novel *in two weeks.* That means that, on average, you'll need to read several chapters a day, including weekends.

Put this on your to-do list for every day, and note on your calendar when you will have finished reading each book.

5. You'll continue breaking down the task this way into planned bits that you can *actually do every day.* Thus the assignment will never get out of control.

You see from this example how such a "daily goals" approach keeps this major assignment—a fifteen-page paper—manageable.

But you also see how important it is to think the project through, break it into smaller bits, and follow through *every day.*

This is the system you'll follow as you plan the entire semester, and it will soon become a productive habit.

When you break tasks down into reachable goals, you're a lot more likely to actually do the work. That's because big projects don't seem so overwhelming when you see them as daily, manageable parts.

Use a "To-Do List" To Beat Procrastination

The second thing you can do to overcome procrastination is also simple. Use a fresh sheet of notebook paper each day to list your assignments and projects.

(Of course, you can use your laptop or phone for this list, and many people rely on Google Calendar, Evernote, or other apps. But many experts still favor paper because it's quicker and you can *check off each item* easily, as it's completed. This is important, and is discussed below.)

Whether you use an app, a spreadsheet, a Word document, or

notebook paper, *the important thing is to build the DAILY habit of using a to-do list!*

On this list, write down ALL assignments for that day. Use the semester's syllabus, plus what the professor adds, to make it current for each class.

There is an old Chinese saying that is relevant here: "The palest ink is stronger than the best memory."

And, as a bonus, you'll find that the daily to-do list is also a stress-reducer. Once you've noted something on your list, there's no need to struggle to keep everything active in your mind. You just look at the list and check off each item as you complete it.

__At the beginning of each item on your to-do list leave a blank underlined space like this for the check-mark you'll use when you complete each task.

__The process of checking each completed entry is important because it demonstrates clearly that you are moving ahead and completing tasks. It's a small visual reward.

This is a simple step—checking off the completed tasks—but it's important. Try it for a few days, and you'll see.

Keep this daily to-do sheet in the front of your notebook (or, of course, you can use your laptop or phone for this purpose if you prefer) and update it with daily assignments.

Do this every day.

Be specific and write legibly.

When using the to-do list becomes a habit, you'll find that you are not in danger of forgetting assignments or falling seriously behind.

That's because this very simple tool is truly *that* powerful.

To repeat: successful business and professional people do this every single day—and there are sophisticated programs and apps for the purpose, too. The point is to have a *written*, up-to-date list of what you need to accomplish each day.

And, as you make your daily list, be specific. For example, don't just write "do algebra." Instead, write, "Do algebra, pp 132-133, 1-25, show work."

You'll also use the to-do list to break down larger assignments, like term papers and book critiques into daily goals, as described above with the Dickens' example.

This really helps you focus on what you need to do each day.

Here's an Example

Here's a sample daily list. Note that it's not just about academic issues. Part of your college life is learning to take care of a wide variety of tasks, and the list is a simple, but surprisingly powerful, tool for accomplishing a lot.

Sample To-Do List

Thursday, October 16

_Read history, pp 15-43

_Type today's history notes

_Do math problems pp 37-38

_Read first 3 chapters of *Heart of Darkness*

_Set up appt w/ Dr. Bernard to discuss idea for sociology paper

_Pick up laundry

_Mail package to Helen

_Get birthday card for Mom

_Go by ATM

Notice that this list includes both daily tasks (like the algebra assignment) and longer-term assignments (such as the *Heart of Darkness* chapters) that are broken down into daily do-able bits.

To repeat, you'll find that it's a small (but very worthwhile) boost and helpful affirmation if you actually check off the items on your list as you finish them. *It's a visual reminder of your progress.*

Please note: this seems like such a simple idea that you may be tempted not to follow through with it, but (like the most successful executives) you'll find that a *written list is a terrific aid to getting things done.*

It's a popular productivity tool . . . because it works!

Now, Reward Yourself

After you complete an assignment or part of a major project, be sure to reward yourself. This can be a big boost to overcoming procrastination.

In fact, an easy way to establish good working habits is to *reward yourself after finishing an important task.* If you regularly do this after completing assignments, you'll soon be in the habit of *doing the work first.*

This is, in fact, a well-researched technique for achieving more, and we'll discuss it in detail later in this book. Give yourself a reward— and it can be a small one—when you have FINISHED a task. It could be as small as going into the kitchen to get a cup of coffee after—not before!—reading a chapter.

So, set the task and think of an appropriate reward. Then do the task and reward yourself.

It's a good habit to build—*work first, but always reward yourself in some way for achievements.*

Be sure, however, to match rewards with the task you've completed. For example, a game of pool in the dorm's commons room might be a good reward for completing a daily reading assignment, while going to a movie or football game may be appropriate for finishing a research paper.

In a Nutshell . . .

So, how do you avoid procrastination and really get started on tasks? You'll be able to really get started on assignments (and finish them!) when you remember to:

Set moderate *daily goals.*

Put assignments on your *to-do list.*

Check off each task as you complete it

Reward yourself when you finish a task.

This is how successful students combat inertia and procrastination. Try it, and you'll see.

PLS Action Step 3

Using a clean sheet of paper, make a to-do list. Leave a space at the beginning of each item to check when it's completed.

Put this daily list in the front of your notebook. Use it to record *each* assignment in *each* class, along with other tasks you need to complete. Do this tomorrow and every day for the rest of the week.

You'll probably have to work at remembering to use this list at first, but you're building a productive habit, and it won't take long for it to become automatic.

To really get the most from your list, check it several times a day, such as before leaving the dorm or your apartment and when you have some free time to sit down and study. That way you won't forget material you need to take with you . . . and you won't forget assignments or errands.

There's nothing worse than getting back to the apartment on a dark, cold, rainy night and realizing that you need to go buy milk or a printer cartridge. Use the list to avoid such stressful moments.

It takes very little time to make and use this kind of list, but when you do your life will be much easier and smoother.

And you'll make visible progress toward your goals *every day*.

PLS Action Step 4

Break a current major assignment (such as a research paper) into realistic daily steps. Write the first step on today's to-do list in your notebook.

Be sure that each day's goal for this project is actually reachable. It is counter-productive to try for unrealistic goals that are just too big.

In fact, good goal-setting requires active thinking.

It's easy to choose a grand-sounding goal, such as "finish the paper," but it's much more effective to do a little planning and make your daily tasks manageable and realistic. If you overreach, this step won't do any good.

So, break the project down into chunks that you can handle and that you'll actually be able to accomplish.

Finally, follow through—and reward yourself when you've completed the task.

Plan to approach your next big project this way, by breaking it down and moving forward every day.

Notice how much smoother the process becomes when you make regular, steady progress.

Chapter 6

Get It Together—How to Organize All That Work

Going to college means you'll be loaded with things to keep up with —textbooks, computers, notebooks, library books, handouts, homework sheets, USB drives, test papers, cellphones, research projects, book critiques, class presentations, and much more.

If you *don't* keep up with these things, you'll waste lots of time searching for lost papers and books. And your grades may suffer.

Have you ever spent time—maybe a lot of time—looking for a missing file on your computer? Or for a missing assignment sheet?

That is *completely lost time*. It's just wasted—thrown away. And if you're trying to be successful in college, you don't have time to waste.

Not only is looking frantically around your apartment for a lost syllabus or library book stressful, it's also time that's simply stolen from your productive hours—there's no other way to put it.

Stolen time. Wasted time.

When you use the *Making A's in College* organizing system, you'll keep your work structured this way:

1. Use the to-do list.

2. Use a three-ring notebook.

3. File papers so you can find them.

4. Devise your own logical computer file system.

5. Have your own "standard places" to keep things.

What you'll be doing, as you repeatedly use these tips, is developing *productive habits*—a powerful way to achieve at a high level. This is not something new. It's been known and practiced for centuries.

Here's a quote from the Greek philosopher Aristotle, who lived about 2300 years ago:

> *We are what we repeatedly do. Excellence,*
> *then, is not an act, but a habit.*

And that's what we're aiming for—excellence—as we build good, productive habits.

Now, here are practical ideas about each one of these organizing techniques.

Using The To-Do List

In addition to helping overcome procrastination, as discussed in chapter five, the to-do list is a terrific tool for getting organized.

Here's how:

1. Use this list (with a calendar) to break down large assignments into daily bits. This is your guide to what *needs to be done today*. Do what highly successful professional people do: *make a daily to-do list and follow it.*

2. Try to get in the habit of quickly checking this list each day before leaving for class, and again before leaving campus for home. This way, you won't forget to take what you need—books, papers, other supplies—nor will you forget what you need to bring home.

3. Many students may prefer to use a computer-based, or phone-based to-do list. If that works for you, it's a good solution.

The key is that the list must be easy to generate, update, and access every single day.

If you get tired of typing several entries into a smartphone's tiny keyboard, it could be that an old-fashioned paper list (perhaps in a small pocket-size notebook) will be a easier and quicker way to keep this list.

High-tech devices are great as you know, but sometimes the easier, most efficient route is the old way. Just choose what works best for you, and use it daily.

The benefits of the to-do list are widely known and taught. If you Google "to-do list and productivity," you'll find hundreds of articles, posts, and videos because *the simple to-do list is one of the most widely-used tools busy people have for getting things done.*

And when you're in college, you're a busy person with lots to do!

So, make and use a daily to-do list. You'll be in the habit in just a few days and you'll wonder how you ever got along without it.

Using the Three-Ring Notebook

This is another traditional study-aid that's been around for generations. But it's effective and efficient, and it will be your study manager. Here's how to set up your notebook for best results.

1. *Don't buy the cheapest notebook*, or the smallest, in the store. Cheap binders won't last through the semester.

2. *Keep your daily to-do list* in the front of the notebook if you like. Since most binders have inside pockets designed for slipping in loose pages, this is the ideal place for your daily list.

3. *Use dividers for each subject*, color-coded if you like. Keep all related material together, including handouts, class outlines, and your own notes.

Thousands of students have wasted millions of hours looking for misplaced handouts, take-home exams, and assignment sheets. Don't you be one of them: put those easy-to-lose pages in your notebook, and when you get back to your room, use a 3-hole punch to put them into the appropriate class section.

4. You may want to *avoid spiral-bound notebooks*. The paper is messy, and the more different notebooks you have, the more likely you are to lose or misplace one. Or forget it. (Of course, when all your notes are in one notebook, be careful not to lose it, and be sure your contact info is written on the inside cover.)

5. *Add a plastic envelope* to your binder for extra supplies such as paper clips, extra pens, colored markers, and so on.

6. *Keep lots of extra paper in your notebook* and a larger supply in your room. Don't miss the crucial part of a lecture because you're trying to borrow paper from a classmate. And since you know you'll use a lot of paper, buy it in larger quantities when it's on sale.

7. *Add a calendar* to the front of your notebook to keep up with big assignments, due dates, holidays, test days, and college events. The big picture—an entire month—is very helpful in planning your time.

Many people, of course, use Google Calendar or something similar, and that's an excellent solution if you prefer. The point is to have an updated calendar always available, always currently updated.

8. *Clean out your notebook frequently.* The end of the term is, of course, the time to file this semester's notes and prepare for the upcoming new classes.

File Papers So You Can Find Them

With all the work you'll be doing in college, you'll benefit from a simple filing system. Follow these suggestions, and you'll be able to locate papers, clippings, old notes, and other important material without searching under the bed or behind your desk.

1. *Set up an official, but simple, file.* You can buy metal or plastic file holders (or just use a cardboard box). A stack of file folders on your desk doesn't count, and neither does a jumble of them stuffed randomly in a desk drawer.

2. *Get a supply of file folders* from a discount store or office supply center. Colored folders are helpful, and you can use different colors for different subjects, which gives you an organizational boost.

Use a separate folder for each subject, or more than one if needed.

3. *Keep anything you think you might need later.* Don't save everything, but think about what's important, what represents a lot of work, and what subjects you're especially interested in.

What would you actually file? Well, you could save:

1. *Papers and reports you've written*. You may be able to use them for notes or references later. Yes, you'll have them on your hard-drive or a USB drive, but a hard copy offers a second level of safety and convenience. When you've spent many hours working on a project, it makes sense to keep it in your files.

2. *Notes you've taken* from an especially interesting professor. You may refer to them later, and if the course was important to you, you may even feel nostalgia for the course in ten or twenty years. Right now, you assume that you'll remember all the details about college, but in a few years you may not even remember the professor's name—or which courses you took.

And you'll probably need to ask professors for a reference letters, as discussed below. It will be easier for them to remember you if you can show the excellent papers you wrote in their classes.

So, file those papers so you can retrieve them later.

3. *Clippings from newspapers and magazines* about subjects you're interested in. If you know you're likely to be writing a paper on the movement of tectonic plates, then watch for interesting articles on geology or earthquakes. Clip and file them, and you may save a lot of research time.

(Evernote, Dropbox or Google Docs and similar apps can be indispensable for saving digital notes and articles, too.)

4. The same thing goes for *websites and urls*. If you run across something especially interesting, at least print out the url so you can find it again. If it's not on a major site, you may even want to print relevant material because web sites come and go.

5. *Mementos from each year of college*, including awards, articles by or about you from the college paper, programs from performances or sports events in which you've participated, special ticket stubs,

awards, college newspaper stories about you, and so on.

College will probably be a highlight of your life, and it's almost certain that you'll look back at these years with nostalgia. So don't discard everything.

6. *Save photos, too*, and if you have a file full of digital photos, back it up on a DVD and put that in your file cabinet or box. Be aware that CDs and DVDs don't last forever, but they'll last for many years, and those photos will become more valuable to you as time passes. You can be sure of that.

Of course, you're likely backing up your phone's photos on Apple's iCloud, Amazon Prime Photos, Google Photos or another cloud-based site. These are good for basic backup, but you can't really assume that the pictures will be there forever. (And find out if such sites are saving full-size or reduced versions of your pictures because it can matter later.)

7. *Official college information.* Save a copy of the catalog, or print relevant financial and academic sections from the college websites. Rules, regulations, and costs change, and you may well need to have easy access to those that apply to you.

You'll find it very useful to also save a printout of each semester's grades in an easy-to-find file. Again, you'll be surprised at how quickly the details fade from your memory.

8. Of course you should save *financial and health records*, including bank statements, receipts for payment to your college, and anything that might affect your taxes. This is a new area of responsibility to many students, so talk with your parents about your taxes and health-care options.

If you've already had the immunizations required by your school, or for international trips, keep those records, too. They can be important in later years and we can guarantee that you won't remember the which shots and boosters you've already had.

9. If you establish a particularly good relationship with a professor, *put his or her name (and pertinent details) in a file.*

It won't be long until you are looking for people to write letters of recommendation, and such a file of names will be very useful.

If you earned an exceptional grade for that presentation on McDonald's marketing in France, for instance, you'd want to keep details about both the presentation and the professor in this file to refresh your memory when you need those important letters of reference.

These are not difficult tasks, at least in theory. But *being organized doesn't come naturally* to many people, and the sudden flood of college work takes many students by surprise. The nine steps above will help you stay in control.

Set up your systems, get in the habit of using them, and you will save much frustration and countless wasted hours.

Use a Logical, Consistent Computer File System

Of course you understand how a computer's document file structure works, but be sure that you devise a system for saving information that makes sense to you.

And, make sure you use it, so *you can find the files you need.*

One very workable, and logical, system is to use a typical nested file structure, setting up a high-level folder for each year, then each semester, and then each class. That way you will be able to find important things three or four (or ten) years from now.

Within the computer document folder for each class, don't just dump files willy-nilly, but be sure to establish folders for different class tasks. Your computer doesn't care how many levels of sub-files you construct, so you could, for instance, have a folder for *American History 101*, and then sub-folders for papers, test prep, class notes, and general information.

You don't need to be obsessive about this, but you *do* need to be able to easily find your files when you need them.

And when your professors email information to you,, or when you find important data on websites, save this info in the relevant file.

The same protocols apply for storing digital photos. Once again, there are several ways to proceed. Some people prefer a strict file-by-date system, while others like a subject folder, and then sub-folders by date.

For example, you may have a sub folder under your "My Pictures" folder, called "Geology Field Trip to Yellowstone" and then subfolders by day or week or subject, depending on how many pictures you make.

If, like many students, you are an avid photographer, you probably have thousands and thousands of digital pictures from your camera and phone.

Cull the poor ones before you waste hard-drive space on then, and then be sure that you can locate the keepers later. If you add an identifying tag or relevant keywords to each batch of photos as you upload to your computer or the cloud, you'll be able to search for them more easily.

Backing Up Isn't Hard to Do (If You're In the Habit)

We point out through this book that *backing up your files is vital*. You surely know that; we all do.

But most people, and especially busy students, don't do a good job of backing up important data.

Bad things can happen to computers—they can be stolen, lost, damaged, struck by lightning or other power surges, infected by viruses. And hard drives can (and do) go bad.

You must protect your college work from this kind of avoidable catastrophe. This isn't rocket science; it's just common sense. Yet, you probably know someone who has lost tons of important files when a hard drive crashed.

In fact, computer experts will tell you that it's not a question of *whether* your hard drive will crash. It's only a question of *when*. (And even solid-state drives and USB thumb drives won't last forever.)

A good strategy is to balance a back-up plan with the amount of work you do on a project (and by how difficult it would be to redo or replace). A one-page book report might not really be a catastrophe if your disk crashes, but a full research paper would certainly be.

We know a doctoral student who lost his *entire* Ph.D. dissertation when his computer was struck by a devastating power surge during a storm. Of course he'd *intended* to back up the file—but he somehow never got around to it. Many months of hard work had to be re-done, and it was a devastating blow.

So buy an external hard-drive. Or two. Use USB drives or SD cards. Email work to yourself. Establish a back-up account in the cloud. Or use Dropbox, Evernote, or Google Drive.

If it's something that's really important to you—perhaps a research paper, maybe your pictures from a semester in Europe—then back up those files in more than one place.

Depending on your operating system, you may already have automatic back-up capability in your computer. If not, there are many easy-to-use programs that make regular backups easy and stress-free. And, if you buy an external hard drive, it will probably come with back-up software installed to make the process easier.

If you haven't done a recent backup, now might be the time to stop reading and do this very important computer maintenance.

Create Your Own "Standard Places" for Things

So, how can you keep from losing things in your dorm room or apartment? How can you keep up with that library book? How can you avoid desperately searching for your keys when you're already late for class?

There's a simple solution. You simply decide WHERE you'll always keep certain things and train yourself to do this every time.

This will quickly become a *productive habit*, and you'll always know where to find your keys, or notebook, or Kindle, or those library books.

In fact, executives go to seminars to learn how to structure their days around productive habits because they know that making some things habitual will save time and increase their efficiency.

So establishing a designated place for certain things is really a common-sense approach, and it will take you very little time to put into action. But you'll have to be intentional about it in the beginning.

First, think about things you have misplaced in the last few weeks and list them on a piece of paper. It could be anything—your checkbook, the incoming mail, class notes, your glasses or sunglasses, your USB drive—anything that tends to get lost around your place.

Then decide WHERE you'll *always* stash these items when you are not using them. Write that down, too. It's usually easy to think of logical places—USB drives could *always* stay in your desk drawer or a small pocket in your backpack.

Library books could *always* stay on the left corner of your desk. Outgoing mail could *always* be by the front door, if there's a table there.

But, be sure to *write down these special places for things*. Make some post-it notes if you need to remind yourself, and then force yourself to follow your own rules of what goes where. This will quickly become a productive habit.

One of the authors of this book had a bad habit of losing parking-lot tickets, and then frantically searching everywhere for that little piece of paper. Did I stick it in my shirt pocket? On the dashboard? In the console? Under the floor mat? Over the sun visor? In my wallet?

Again, this is not rocket science, but once I decided to ALWAYS put parking-lot tickets behind the bills in my wallet, I've never had to search for the ticket while cars wait impatiently behind me and the cashier glares at me for holding up the line.

It was a simple change, but it's saved me lots of frustration.

This organizational technique is simple, but effective. If you'll make it a habit to *always* keep certain things in the same places, you'll save a lot of time and avoid a lot of unnecessary stress.

PLS Action Step 5

What are your organizational weak points? Have you lost papers or library books? Are you in the habit of backing up your hard drive and saving files to multiple locations? Is your desk or dorm room a danger zone?

Do these things before class tomorrow:

1. Clean out and organize your notebook. Use dividers for each class.

2. Be sure your to-do list is in place for easy use.

3. Buy file folders and devise a place to store them—a file cabinet, desk drawer or even a sturdy cardboard box. Label the folders and start your file system.

4. Think about your computer's file system and decide what basic structure you'll use.

5. Back up your hard drive. If you need to buy an external hard-drive or sign up for an online backup account, do it this week. This is almost guaranteed to be money and time well spent.

6. Decide where you'll keep the things you tend to misplace most often. Make post-it notes to remind yourself of your new designated places for these items until you've created productive habits.

Chapter 7

Time Marches On—But You Can Manage It

Do you have trouble finding time to study? Here's why:

You're *in class* about 15-20 hours a week.

You may have *club meetings and activities.*

There may be sports *practices and games.*

Perhaps you have *band rehearsals or music lessons.*

There are *duties at the dorm* or your apartment.

Possibly you have *a part-time job.*

Of course you have *social activities.*

Social media takes a sizeable chunk of every day.

It takes time to get to and from class .

And after all, you do *have to sleep.*

Here's a well-established rule of thumb for college students who are working toward good grades: **you should expect to study on your own two hours for each hour of class time.** Thus, a class that meets three hours a week would require six hours of outside study.

Of course that's just an average. Very difficult classes such as accounting or chemistry, to name only two, might need much more outside study time.

.

The main point to remember is that for successful students *time in class is only the beginning.*

When you add in the hours many students spend checking email, Facebook, YouTube, Instagram and surfing the web, you can see that learning to control your time is very important.

That's why time-management skills are so crucial. Do a little multiplication and you'll quickly see that this is going to be a very important need in college.

Many college students suffer from the too-much-of-a-good-thing syndrome. Often there are just too many worthwhile and fun activities, and that leaves little time for studying. Each activity—sports, clubs, dates, social groups, computer games, hanging out with friends, updating social media, or whatever—is good in itself, but the overall effect is that *you can run out of time.*

Here's the Bottom Line

Here's the bottom line: *you have to plan your study time.* It won't just happen.

This, in fact, is the main point made by Elizabeth, a law student, and Chris, a medical student, in their interviews in chapter 17. College students have many demands on their time but *when you use these time-management techniques, you'll get more done.*

Maybe you'll even have time left over.

Here are hands-on tips for getting control of the hours and minutes of your day. (And it's true, *even minutes are important.*)

First, Look at Where Your Time Goes

1. *Make a sample block schedule* to see where the time goes. For this chart, don't try to record every minute, but just put down the big chunks of time like classes, athletic events, jobs, and social plans.

At this point you want to get an *overview* of where the blocks of time are being used each day. This process is described in the next *PLS* step.

2. Now, *use the diary that you created in PLS step 2 to record your internet and media use.* Do this for several days to get an accurate picture. Record your time on the computer, on social-networking sites, time spent emailing, texting, on Twitter, Tumblr, Snap, and so on.

Include the time you spend watching TV and chatting on the phone, too.

This will give you an idea—often a surprising view—of how much time you spend in fun, but not really vital, activities. It can be an eye-opener, and may lead you to make some adjustments that will give you a lot more productive time in your days, with very little effort.

Please understand: we're NOT saying that these activities are bad or that you should stop using your favorite social media sites.

What we ARE saying is that, to succeed in college (and later in life, too), you really must be in control of your time.

You'll get a lot more accomplished if you aren't trying to divide your attention in several directions. So first, to make improvements in your productivity, you have to know where your time goes now.

Now, Decide WHEN You Can Study

Now, use the twelve techniques below to find more time in your day.

1. *Use small bits of time* when you have them. Don't wait until you have a full hour to study; use fifteen minutes here and ten minutes there.

Can't think of the best way to spend those extra, spare minutes? Check your to-do list—it will remind you.

These little bits of time add up, and often studying in small segments can be more efficient anyway.

2. *Keep something productive to do in your backpack*, such as a book you're reading. If you take notes on flash cards, it's easy to keep a few of them with you. Then when you're stuck in traffic or waiting at the bus stop, you can get some studying done.

To repeat, these minutes can add up quickly.

3. *Use a calendar to get an overview* of the semester's big projects and due dates. This is not the same as your to-do list because the calendar is where you keep up with the *big picture* of what you have to do.

A large wall calendar or a monthly calendar in your binder will quickly show this at a glance. Just be sure there is room to write on the space for each day. Tiny, or photo-filled, calendars may not be practical for this purpose.

Many people swear by Google Calendar, and it is a very handy to keep synchronized information on your devices. But some people still like to see a constant reminder on a big wall-calendar.

Find your own best calendar approach—digital or physical--and use it diligently to keep up.

4. Now that you have a calendar and the big picture in mind, *work backward from due dates* to break big projects down into manageable bits, often called "chunks," and establish a timeline for your projects. For example, if a book review is due Friday the 15th, you might think like this:

_The review must be emailed to the professor by noon on the 15th, so I must get it typed and proofed. I should be sure it's all finished and checked over by the 14th.

_Since I usually have a hard time writing papers, I need to be working on this assignment by the 10th. I know it will take me a couple of days to think it through and get a decent paper written.

_That means that I need to have finished reading the book by the 9th or earlier if possible. It would also be good to do some online research about the author and to read a couple of critical essays for background.

_That means I need to start reading the book by the 4th so I'll have 5 days.

_I need to check the library tomorrow. If the book isn't available, I need to go to the bookstore or download the ebook edition.

Does that seem like a lot of work? It's really not—it's a process of thinking about a project as *a series of smaller, logical steps*, and noting *when* you need to finish each step.

This approach really doesn't add work, but it will save you time and frustration because you'll be in control of what you need to do.

5. *Focus on what's most important.* If you have a term paper due that is worth half your grade, be sure to give it the attention it deserves.

Don't get lost in the tangle of daily assignments (but don't ignore them either—just be sure to give the larger project the larger part of your time).

6. To be specific, *rank the items on your to-do list in order of their importance.* Work on the big things first.

7. Since you know from the diary of your media time (item number two on this list, above) how much time you spend with electronic media daily, resolve that when you are busy with schoolwork, you'll limit your TV and media time.

All the social networks and constant texting can wait—they'll still be there in an hour or two. *Think about what's really important* when you're running short on time, and act.

8. *Don't procrastinate.* Go ahead and *do something* on big projects. Often, just getting started is the hardest step, so use your to-do list, and break down larger, challenging assignments as described in chapter three.

Don't try to do everything at once. But get started by *doing something today.* And do something else on the same project tomorrow. And the next day. Soon, you'll be well along toward completing the project . . . but you have to get started by *doing something.*

9. *Keep up with books, papers, and assignments.* Time spent looking for lost material is wasted. It's time thrown away, and for no reason.

If you share a room or apartment with others, decide where you'll keep your books, your school supplies, and so on, and get in the habit of keeping them in that assigned place, as described in chapter six.

That way, you won't be looking under the couch, or in the kitchen, or under your roommate's car seat for your calculus book.

10. Make a *Studying! Do Not Disturb!* sign, and use it when you're studying. Try it before you dismiss this idea—lots of students find that it's really helpful in claiming some real study time.

Of course you want to be able to visit with your friends, but it's better (and more satisfying, too) to *get your work done first* and then socialize. Ask your roommates for their cooperation, or if necessary, plan to do your studying in the library.

Interruptions break your train of thought and destroy your concentration. It will take time to get back in the "studying mood" after an interruption, so it's simpler and more efficient to find ways to avoid these intrusions into your study time.

11. *Learn to read more effectively.* Just think of the time you'll save if you don't have to re-read the thousands of pages you'll cover as you go through college. The **PART** reading system, described in chapter 11, is a simple but very effective way to make your reading better.

You may never have thought about how well you read, but *for most college students, even a small improvement in reading speed and efficiency can make a huge difference in time spent on assignments.*

12. *Develop and use a backup strategy* for your files. This is a repeated theme through this book, but it's too easy to ignore, or to put off until tomorrow. You doubtlessly know someone who has a terrible computer disaster story, and those stories come in many types. Most of them could be avoided with good, frequent backups.

The bottom line, as you certainly know, is that any mechanical or electronic device will fail at some point. *Every one.* So the smart thing to do is be prepared.

Does it make sense to trust your valuable data, and all your hard work, to a hard drive that is *destined* to fail at some unknown point in the future? Of course not.

So devise a backup plan and stick to it. Make it routine to back up your documents, photos, and whatever is important. To be really safe, keep a copy of your backup in a second location, too.

If you don't control time, it will control you. Do what high-achievers in all fields do, and take these steps to be sure you don't waste this most valuable, and fleeting, resource.

PLS Action Step 6

Make a sample schedule for yourself and keep it for a week. Make a basic time grid from a sheet of paper by writing the days of the week in columns across the top, and listing each hour on the vertical axis along the left side.

Don't try to record everything you do, or track every minute, but write down the big things—classes, jobs, meetings, home or dorm tasks, and scheduled events. In other words, *block out, on this grid, the time in your week that is already taken by a defined, scheduled activity.* You might even color in the blocks that are already committed for greater visual impact.

This will be a striking view of where your time goes, (and this chart doesn't even include the media time we discussed above.)

Now, *use a different colored marker to select the times that are available for you to study*. It will almost certainly be a lot less than you would have expected.

Next, ask this important question, "Is there enough time available for me to study? Or is my daily time already fully taken with other activities?"

Use this weekly chart to get an overall feel for whether your time is balanced, or whether you need to do some serious thinking about what is important.

Once you've identified the times that are *available* for studying in your busy week, also ask yourself this question: do the times that are available for studying match my own *prime time*, the periods when I'm most alert?

Try to block out some study time each day when you are most energized and at your best, because that will vary during the day. We'll talk about your personal "prime time" in chapter eight.

When you look at this simple schedule, illustrating the time that is already taken by your activities, you'll have a clear picture of why time management is so important for college students.

Chapter 8

How to Build Your Concentration

If your mind wanders in class or you have trouble focusing on studying, you need to improve your ability to concentrate. In fact, this may be your most important college—and life—skill as the world becomes more complex each year.

The truth is that students today may have a more difficult time concentrating because of the explosion of electronic gadgets and tools, and the *constant* presence of so many alluring distractions.

In today's digital world, we expect immediate results. It's the new norm. We expect to multi-task. We normally do several things at once.

But when it comes to studying, we need to stop and ask: is this the best approach to learning effectively and efficiently?

Here's an example of how our normal approach works.

We usually follow links in a random way when we're online. When something looks interesting, we click a link, and off we go in a new direction. This happens over and over until we've lost our original train of thought and wasted a lot of time.

Sometimes this approach is compared to a spider-web, with links branching out in many different directions. Sometimes it's called "networked thinking," and many times it's useful as a way to find unexpected connections.

Often, though, it becomes a distracting time-trap, because all those links are so interesting, alluring, and accessible.

Why FOCUS Is So Important in College

In college, you'll find that random link-following may not be very productive.

In fact, you'll often have to think in the more traditional "linear" way, where you move from *a to b,* and then to *c* and *d.* It's an orderly way of thinking, with one fact building on another and leading to a logical conclusion.

Sometimes, when we are used to quickly leaping from link to link and site to site, this more traditional way of learning seems painfully slow. For many students, it's difficult to switch from the fast pace of the internet entertainment to the much slower pace of the textbook and lecture hall.

Truthfully, your professors won't often be as exciting as a fast-moving web experience.

But here's the main point of this chapter: *surfing the web may not be as helpful to your grades this semester (or your future success), as paying attention to a lecture or a textbook,* even if the lecture and book are not as fast-paced as a Netflix series or video game.

It's important to remember that lectures and reading are still where most learning takes place, and *in college you'll really need to be able to focus for extended periods of time.*

If your concentration is poor, you may find yourself spending much more time than necessary as you study. And, often you won't learn what you should.

You may feel that you are simply going through the motions, but not really getting ahead, not really learning.

So, you'll do your college career a BIG favor if you learn to focus your concentration sharply.

And you can.

Sometimes You ARE Completely Focused

Interestingly, there *are* times when you focus completely on what you're doing and your concentration is at a peak. When? Typically, when you're playing sports, playing a musical instrument, or playing a video game.

What is it about these activities that allows you to focus your attention completely on them?

When you think about it, you realize that in these situations, you are *actively involved*. You're *a participant*. You are engaged, and your mind is *in gear.*

What's more, you're *enjoying what you are doing.*

If you can approach studying the same way, being active and making it enjoyable, your concentration will automatically improve. So, our main effort will be to *help you become an active student*, not just going through the motions, but deeply involved in learning.

Our goal is to help you study with your mind actively in gear.

Four Ways to Be Active When You Study

So, here are four ways to study actively:

1. *Study by the question and answer method.* This forces your mind to be active.

As you study, challenge the author. Pretend you're the professor. Ask questions as you move through the chapter, and see if you can answer them.

A quick way to formulate good questions is to turn chapter headings, subheads, and picture captions into questions. If a subhead in a Greek history book is *The Lelantine War and the Emergence of Corinth,* you could ask, "What was the Lelantine War?" and "How did it affect Corinth?"

Creating these questions won't be too difficult. Answering them may be, but take your time. Difficult material, especially, may go more slowly and require real concentration, but this is the way to learn.

Read, question, and think about what you're learning. Will it slow you down? Yes, in the short run, because it simply takes more time to think about what you're reading.

But with this method *you'll actually be learning the material*, and not just running your eyes down the page. Try it and see.

2. *Make flash cards.* This is a refinement of the question-and-answer technique discussed above. These inexpensive little cards can be the basis for a powerful study system. We'll describe this in more detail later, but it's another form of active learning.

To make a flash card, write a term, word, phrase, question, or formula on one side of the card. The answer goes on the back. You'll be *actively leaning* as you MAKE the cards, and as you USE them.

Thus, making flash cards is an easy two-for-one study bonus.

3. *Talk to yourself* about what you're studying. Walk around the room and explain the subject out loud. Teach it to yourself, or teach it to someone else. If you can find a study group, you can talk to other people about the subject, and this is a good active learning method.

But if you don't have a good study group, talk to yourself. Seriously. This is an excellent strategy for staying active as you study—talk out loud if no one is around, or "talk" to yourself silently.

4. *Relate the subject to other events in your life* or in the news. Learning doesn't take place in a vacuum. Calculus, biology, and history will be more interesting when they're related to events in the world.

So always look for connections, correlations and contrast with outside events.

One more thing: to focus actively on the task at hand, to be present in the moment, you must not allow yourself to be distracted by the usual suspects—email, cellphone, social media, Instagram, YouTube, and television.

To repeat, it's not that these things are your enemy, but you need to put them aside while you study.

Your time is most valuable when you use it wisely and that means, simply, to study actively when you study.

Don't allow your valuable, precious study time to be compromised by other things. Distractions can wait, and they will.

Your studying cannot.

Enjoy Studying and Learning

Many good students would agree that little in life is as exhilarating as truly learning something new or really mastering a subject. The world is an endlessly fascinating place and your basic job as a college student is to learn about that intriguing world.

In fact, this may be the last time in your life that you can devote so much time to just learning a broad range of things without worrying too much about practicality. So enjoy it!

One way to enjoy studying is to devise games, puzzles, and contests. Study with a friend to get the full benefit of these techniques, but you can also "play" against yourself. See how much you can learn and keep score. Test yourself against a friend or study partner.

Building on that idea is the excellent technique of finding good study partners to work with. Many graduate schools rely on the study group technique, but you can form your own group, even if it's only two people.

Discuss, question, research and work together to master new and difficult material.

Often this is an unbeatable study technique, but you must be careful not to make it just a social occasion. When you are studying in a group, be sure to stay targeted on your purpose; it's easy to get distracted and just waste time (and you don't have extra time to waste). Laura D, a medical student interviewed in chapter 17, makes this point very clearly.

Finally, to make studying enjoyable, try to choose subjects you're interested in for research papers and projects, extra reading reports, and group projects. When there is a choice, pick a topic that intrigues you. Why be bored?

So, *being active* as you study and *making learning enjoyable* are two powerful ways to improve your concentration. But there are other strategies you can use to help focus.

More Ways to Improve Your Concentration

Reduce distractions when you're studying. Digital devices, television and video are often big offenders.

Remember the research discussed earlier about multi-tasking and don't squander your time by watching a movie or ballgame while you study.

It's more efficient and less frustrating to study for a while and then watch the movie. This way, you'll get more out of each activity.

Recent research confirms that most Americans spend nearly 35 hours a week just watching television, an all-time high. That's almost equivalent to a full-time job, and it raises an obvious question: *what's NOT getting done during those couch-potato hours?*

Over the years, I've had several students tell me that *simply turning off the TV while studying was the biggest single thing they did to help their grades.* It seems simple, and in a way it is, though the TV (and, of course, internet) habit can be very hard to break.

Once again, remember that digital devices, in general, are very alluring and habit-forming. To focus on what's important—whether it's college now, a job later, or a personal relationship—you must learn to control your devices. Remember: YOU are the boss, not your phone, tablet, or any social media.

You would think it's pretty obvious, wouldn't you, that you can't learn difficult material with the television competing for your attention. It's equally obvious that you can't expect to grasp abstract math concepts, for example, with your phone competing for your mental bandwith.

It is crucial to understand that all our media experiences are *designed to be addictive*, to hold our attention so we'll watch the commercials, It can be very difficult to stand up to the powerful forces that want our eyeballs, minds, time, (and money.)

Here's something you can try right now: if you've been in the habit of trying to study in front of the TV. Try turning it off.

You may find that this one change really improves your grades.

One student I know took a more radical step to solve his television problem. About a year after he had attended one of my study-skills seminars, I ran into him on campus. He thanked me for the seminar, and told me that he had come to the seminar because he was on academic probation and in danger of flunking out of the university.

But, this last semester, he added, smiling, he was on the Dean's List.

"What made that much difference?" I asked. "What did you do?"

He said, "Simple. I sold my TV."

You may not want to go quite that far, but *you will find it very helpful to take positive steps to limit your media time.*

It will really help your grades.

Don't Let Digital Distraction Rob You

Learn to control your online social networks so YOU, and not digital devices, are in charge of your future.

I've discussed this before and will again, because phones, laptops and other digital devices are a constant part of all our lives. You will learn better and more quickly if you don't constantly interrupt yourself to check email or to text your friends. This can be a *huge* problem, and online distraction often becomes a real addiction.

Think about this: if you don't control digital distraction, it will control you.

In fact, working to control digital distraction is a favorite technique of Laura G, another successful student interviewed in chapter 17. And, productivity blogs often feature helpful articles on how to control the email monster because it's now a worldwide problem for businesses, too.

You can even buy apps and programs that will restrict your internet access if you can't control it yourself. Popular ones include *Anti-Social, Freedom App, TrackTime, Concentrate*, and *StayFocused*. You'll find these, and others, in your app store.

But you may not need to go that far.

Perhaps the most direct way to counter the temptation to constantly check these devices is to set aside study time, spend that block of time studying (without so much as glancing at your phone or computer), and then reward yourself by checking email or Instagram *after* that block of studying is done.

Many students (and executives, too), simply set a timer and work until it rings. I'll repeat a useful phrase: *work first, then have a small reward. Then work again.*

You'll find that your friends are still there on social media, and that you can spend substantial amounts of time offline with no ill effects in order to accomplish your bigger goals.

(And, if you simply can't muster the determination to block out the internet while you study, the apps listed above will literally do it for you. Even if you don't think you need these apps, have a look at them in your app store to see what's available. You'll be surprised at how widespread this problem is.)

Reduce Distractions at School

Reduce distractions at school. Sit as close to the front of each class as you can. You'll see the monitor or board better, hear the lecture better, and won't be distracted by other students. Research clearly shows that students who sit near the front of the class do better, and it's easy to see why.

Studies also show that students who text during class, or fiddle with their digital devices, not only harm their own class performance, but *they affect nearby students as well.* Simply moving toward the front of the class will avoid this needless distraction.

Create a study center at home or in the dorm. This is a major part of your *PLS*, so gather materials and supplies together in one place where you won't be disturbed as you study. Get your roommate's help, if possible.

You'll study *much* better at a desk or a table than on the floor or in bed. So find a place you can set up as your office or study center. Since *college is really your job right now*, it may help to literally think of this area as your official office.

You may have to search to locate such a place to study. Unfortunately, many dorms aren't particularly suitable, and your roommates may not share your desire to succeed—or their class and test schedules may be different from yours.

But finding a distraction-free place to study is important to your new study ritual, so spend some time and find a good place that suits your study style.

Often an excellent solution is to study in the library. Check to see if your school's library assigns study carrels or has lockers available for you to use.

Even if you can't claim such an "official" spot in the library, you can often find a particularly quiet corner somewhere in the building. If you go to that same table each time you're settling in to study, it will quickly become associated in your mind with effective study, and will actually help you quickly get in the right frame of mind.

Some college libraries have a designated "silent floor" where talking is prohibited. One of the students we interviewed for chapter 17, Breen, says that such a specified floor was "crucial" to his college success because he finds that he is easily distracted by conversation, music and ambient sounds.

(Interestingly, several of the successful students we interviewed for chapter 17, pointed out that *simply going to the library is not enough to avoid distractions*. One, Laura D., finds that many students congregate at large tables in her medical-school library, and their talking makes it hard to concentrate on serious study.

So, she says "hello" to the group, and then finds a quieter spot on an upper floor for her studying.)

Good Habits Can Make It Easier

Establish a study ritual. By approaching your study time the same way each day, you'll build a productive routine that will quickly improve your concentration.

There is a lot of interest today in building productive habits, and Stephen Covey's best-selling book *The 7 Habits of Highly Successful People* is just one example of many. Building a good study routine, and finding a special place to study is is one useful habit you should try to create soon.

I've worked with many students who use a ritual to get in the mood to study. One takes off her bracelets so the jangling won't disturb her. Another student removes everything from his desktop but the book he's working on. Several students like to start a study session with a soft drink or a cup of coffee.

Many students go to the same place every day for their best study time because they've associated that place with feeling productive. Every day, they go to the same library nook or coffee shop, open their books, and plunge right in.

This way, a ritual can be a *productive habit* that puts you quickly in the mood to study. Establish a daily pattern, follow it, and before long, you'll be almost addicted to doing your work.

Planning in advance for study time is an effective strategy many students use to help them concentrate as they study. These students often find that pre-planning a definite time for reading or review helps guarantee that it will take place.

It's somehow easier to push aside distractions when you've scheduled a block of time that you expect to spend studying. In fact, this is a major point made by Chris, a medical student, in chapter 17.

This is another advantage—and a big one—of the to-do list we discussed in Chapter Six. Just put your block of study time on your daily list and check it off when you've finished studying.

Have the tools and supplies you need. If you run out of copy paper while you're working on the final draft of a research paper, you're not studying smart.

Your study center doesn't need to be elaborate, but it should have everything you need. That could include paper, pencils, pens, blank DVDs or CDs, extra ink or laser cartridges, pencil sharpener, 3-hole punch, and so on.

You don't need the unnecessary distraction of interrupting a crucial study session to rush to the office-supply store and search for the right cartridge for your printer. And if you plan ahead just a bit, you can order online easily and quickly.

Office supplies and computer consumables remind me of gas in a car. If you don't replenish each in a timely way, you'll run out (and usually at the worst possible time).

Your car won't re-fill itself with gas, and your printer *will* need more ink or toner.

Simplify your life and reduce your stress by planning ahead.

See the Finish Line Just Ahead

Challenge yourself. Give yourself a deadline to focus your concentration. Tell yourself that you *will have finished reading* a difficult chapter before you go out for the evening, and stick to that plan.

Then, when you go out, you'll feel better because you will have met your own study challenge.

And be specific with these self-challenges. Say, for instance, "I know I can learn this theorem in 20 minutes." Then time yourself, and at the end of twenty minutes, test yourself to see.

Again, small goals work better than large ones. This is a very useful way to stay focused and concentrating: set a goal, reach it, test yourself quickly, and move on.

Study at your prime time. You can't study effectively when you're tired or drowsy, so plan study sessions for your best, most alert hours. If you put off studying until the end of the day when your energy is depleted, it will take longer—perhaps much longer—and won't be very efficient.

Different people obviously have different peak times for studying, and you should think about how your energy ebbs and flows during the day to find your best time.

Some students, believe it or not, get up early to study first thing in the morning, and they tell me that they learn much more at that time of day, when there are fewer distractions and they are at their peak of alertness.

Some studies indicate that many people are less alert—even sleepy—in the afternoon right after lunch, so this may not be your best time for study. The bottom line is that you should experiment a bit to *find out when you're most alert*, and then try to match it with your study schedule.

When you try to work *with* your body's alertness cycle rather than *against* it, you'll be studying smarter, and not harder. And you'll learn more in less time, too.

Keep your goals in sight. You know you're working toward the very worthwhile goals of making A's in college, opening doors to what lies ahead, and learning as effectively as you can. Keeping the target in front of you will make it easier to reach.

Doing well in college isn't easy, and it really shouldn't be. Most worthwhile things, as you have learned, take work and often are difficult to achieve. Any coach will tell you the same thing. But your efforts to do well will be rewarded.

Sometimes, when it's hard to focus, when you need to study but would rather be somewhere else, it can be particularly difficult to force yourself to do the work you have in front of you. That happens to everyone. There's always something fun just waiting for you, isn't there?

Why Am I Here?

But this the time that you should stop and think for a minute about *why you're in college at all, and why it's important to do well.*

Remind yourself often that what you're doing, hard as it may be, is really worthwhile. In fact, it will likely determine the fate of the rest of your life.

Remember: *good grades bring recognition, fulfillment, admission to preferred graduate schools, possible scholarships, and more.*

And high GPA's often have a direct impact on after-graduation job offers. Don't forget, either, that the higher your educational achievement, the higher your income will likely be, and the more choices you'll have later in life. Study after study confirms the direct link between college success and lifetime income.

Building concentration is a vital success skill. This is particularly true today when we live in a virtual sea of high-powered distractions. If you remember the tips from this chapter and put them to work in your study life, you'll do better in school.

And if you *don't* build your ability to concentrate, you'll work harder, longer, and achieve less.

College is likely costing you and your family a lot of money, and when you improve your ability to concentrate, you'll get more value for all that tuition.

And, that's a guarantee.

PLS Action Step 7

This is a two-part *PLS* activity.

First, Think!

First, to build your concentration, think about anything that stands in your way. What keeps you from focusing on your work?

Snapchat?

Texting?

TV?

Facebook?

Twitter?

Email?

Vine?

Phone conversations?

Online games?

Hanging out with friends?

Using the ideas from this chapter and the digital distraction inventory from *PLS Action Step 2, make a list of the steps you can take NOW to improve your concentration.* Again, this list is for you alone to see and work with, so be honest.

Most students really do understand that distractions are devastating for their study time, but many never honestly confront this problem because it isn't easy to admit.

And that means that too many students don't take direct steps to control the distractions.

But you can, you should, and you really must. The ability to concentrate is so vital to your college success that it's a logical place to start in building strong college success skills.

As you make this list of what you need to do to improve concentration, be specific. So, don't write, "Cut down on TV." Instead, write, "Only watch my two favorite programs on Tuesday and Thursday nights AFTER I've finished my work for the day."

That way, your resolution has concrete meaning and is something you'll act on.

Let's go one step further with this example of something you might include in your *building concentration* list.

Don't just write "Quit studying in front of the TV." Instead, find a place to study that is *away* from the television. That's being *proactive* as you take control of your time, and it will work.

In other words, don't just randomly think about where you might study away from electronic distractions. Instead, *make a plan and write it down.*

Now, Act!

The second part of this *PLS Action Step*, is to take whatever steps you need to arrange your own schedule and study space so you can make it easier to concentrate.

Do you need to make changes in the time of day you typically study? When are you most alert? When do you tend to feel sleepy?

If your dorm or apartment isn't conducive to study, you might need to make a portable study center in a backpack, with the supplies you need for studying. Take it with you to the library, a friend's room, a coffee shop, or wherever you can concentrate effectively.

A USB drive will enable you to carry the files you're working on to any computer you're using, and that can be very handy. (Always use your anti-virus program to scan this USB drive, though, if you use it on 'foreign' computers. USB drives are notorious carriers of hidden viruses and trojan malware, so remember to be on guard if you move a drive from computer to computer.)

In this *PLS* step, you have developed your own plan to overcome the distractions you encounter, and you have found a good time and a good place to study. These are big, useful steps to take.

Now, you're set to use all the practical tips from this chapter to improve your concentration.

Practice these ideas *each day* in class, in the dorm, or at home until they become habits, and you'll see your study efficiency improve dramatically.

Chapter 9

How Your Memory Works (and Why It Sometimes Doesn't)

Have you ever studied for hours . . . and forgotten it all when you sat down two days later to take an exam?

Or, have you read several chapters but not been able to remember anything at all from them—*as soon as you closed the book*?

These memory problems can often be solved by understanding a bit about how memory works and using that knowledge in a practical way.

So this chapter gives you pertinent information from research labs that you can actually use today to improve your grades.

Understanding how your memory works is essential to the *Making A's in College* note-taking, reading, and studying systems that we'll describe in later chapters.

It may seem theoretical, but acting on this research-based knowledge will almost immediately improve your study habits and retention of new material you've studied. This relatively simple technique will be really helpful to almost all students.

Even if it seems that our study suggestions require more time, you'll actually save time in the long run because you remember so much more. You do that by working *with* your memory rather than *against* it.

We All Have Two Kinds of Memory

First, psychologists and researchers divide memory into two types.

Each type has a different function, and it is crucial to understand how these two kinds of memory work. That's because, once you visualize the basic idea of *how memory works*, our study and reading strategies will make perfect sense.

In fact, these strategies are built on this understanding.

Short-term memory (also often called *working memory*) has limited capacity and only lasts for a brief time. This kind of memory is useful for the kinds of things you don't need to remember for long, such as a new street address you might be looking for.

Have you ever gotten a new friend's phone number and remembered it long enough to enter it into your phone's contacts app or address book? That's your *short-term memory* at work, but if you forgot to enter the new number, or didn't write it down, chances are very good that you couldn't remember it later that day.

The limitation of this short-term memory for study is obvious, isn't it? Short-term memory won't help you remember all the new facts and figures you'll be learning in college because of the way it functions.

Brain scientists have a more complex description, of course, but for our purposes it's useful to think of this short-term memory as a limited, temporary "holding area" for things that we may not need to remember for a long time.

So, how *does* short-term memory relate to your learning? What does knowing about short-term memory have to do with improving your grades?

Here's why it's relevant. When you are reading, short-term memory enables you to remember the beginning of the sentence so it connects to the end of that sentence and makes sense. Or, to extend that example, short-term memory enables you to remember the main idea of a paragraph and relate it to the details within it.

(In other words, short-term memory enables you to comprehend what you're reading, and it enables you to follow a lecture and remember what you've heard long enough to get it down in your notes.)

So it's clear that short-term memory is uscful and essential. But this kind of memory is not designed to remember things for a long time. This kind of memory *very limited*—that's the way it's designed— and it's limited in two ways.

First, short-term memory simply can't hold very much information. Too much input all at once, and it will be overwhelmed.

Second, research has shown that new information doesn't stay in the short-term memory very long.

So, our short-term memory is limited in both capacity and duration.

And you're learning a lot of things that you must remember for a long time.

That's obviously a problem, isn't it?

Think Of a Quart Jar

An example will help make this point clear, and it helps to visualize your short-term memory as a quart jar.

That jar has limited capacity and *when you've filled it up, it holds no more water*. Anything more that's poured in will just overflow. (In the original video version of this book, I poured water into a quart jar to illustrate this point clearly.)

Your short-term memory is like that quart jar.

Like the jar, it has a limited capacity and when it's full, it simply can't hold any more information. *Too much* new information is a problem.

Thus, *too much* information coming into your memory without pause will simply overload it.

And, new information coming into your short-term memory *too fast* is also a problem.

Here's what that means for you: when you are learning new material, your task is to move—and move quickly!—that new information from your short-term memory into your permanent, long-term memory.

Here's the Memory Solution

Fortunately, long-term memory is different from the short-term memory we just described. It has much larger—maybe even unlimited—capacity.

Information in this kind of memory can last for a long, long time—even a lifetime.

But—information doesn't flow directly into this longer-term memory. *It must first pass through, and be processed by, your limited, short-term memory system*. Once you understand this important point about how your memory works, the study strategies in this book will make perfect sense to you.

So, to remember what you're learning, information in short-term memory must be converted to long-term memories. This is a process that psychologists call *consolidation,* but you don't need to know the name for the process—you just need to know how to use it!

Let's Put This New Knowledge to Work

The trick, then, and the key to remembering a lot of new information, is to move it from short-term to long-term memory effectively. *Here are two simple, but vital steps you can take to help your brain make that all-important transfer of information.*

First, don't overload your short-term memory, or all that new information will simply "overflow" as it would from over-filling a quart jar with water. You must give your working memory *time* to process new information by stopping frequently as you study to *think about what you're learning.*

This is also why multi-tasking isn't helpful when you are studying. Your brain literally doesn't know what to do with all the different, unrelated, often high-speed bits of information that are assaulting it, so it simply doesn't do a good job with any of it.

(If you'd like to know more about the latest research in this area, do an internet search on "multitasking + human brain." It's an active field of study and you'll find plenty of interesting stories.)

Second, to help make the transfer to long-term memory, it is very helpful to *rehearse* new information by repeating it to yourself and thinking about it. This gives the brain the *time* it needs to process new information and "store" it properly.

A very readable, but more detailed, explanation of this process (and many others) can be found in the book *Brain Rules*, by Dr. John Medina, a developmental molecular biologist at the University of Washington School of Medicine. If you are interested in current understanding of how your brain actually works, you'll enjoy his book.

Dr. Medina calls the process of repeating and adding details to what we've learned or experienced "elaborative rehearsal." This is the crux of the matter—*it is the most effective way to really remember information for a long time.*

For example, if you hear a joke and then tell it to someone else, perhaps adding your own twists and details, you are much more likely to remember the joke a few days later.

Why?

Because your retelling the joke soon after you learned it (and adding a few more details) is a form of "elaborative rehearsal."

When you retold that joke, you were really "rehearsing" it, and helping make it more permanent in your memory.

In other words, you're much more likely to remember this joke because you've gone over the joke, added to it, maybe repeated it a couple of times to yourself. After that process, you'll probably remember it.

And that's the point.

Learning important new information works exactly the same way.

To Remember New Information, Rehearse It

The rehearsal step is crucial. It's the key, and that's why it is central to the active study techniques described in the rest of this book.

This is so important that it needs to be repeated!

**The rehearsal step is CRUCIAL
in really learning new information.**

So, don't simply throw a huge mass of new data at your brain and expect to remember it the next day or the next week.

Think about it (actively) as you read or listen, and *then go over it again* (rehearse it) in your mind, and perhaps in your notes.

It's the act of rehearsing the material a second or third (or more) time that gets it into your long-term memory where you want it to be.

Here's The Key to Efficient Learning In A Nutshell

For many students, this simple tip will be the most important one in this book so let's repeat it for emphasis.

To remember new material for a long time (that is, to move it from short- to long-term memory), ACTIVELY go over it in your mind by rehearsing, repeating, thinking or talking about it, or taking notes.

If you try for one-pass learning, like reading a chapter in history without stopping, you'll almost certainly not recall what you've read for very long because you've skipped the "rehearsal" step. *The rehearsal step is crucial.*

Does it take more time to stop and think or take notes on what's important to remember?

Perhaps in the short run it does because you are deliberately pondering as you read and study. However, in the big picture, you'll be learning more effectively and efficiently, and you'll probably be learning faster than before. You'll certainly be learning better!

If you aren't sure you understand this important point, take the time to re-read the first part of this chapter on how memory works because this is the key to the *Making A's in College* approach to effective, efficient learning.

Rehearsal Combats Forgetting

Now, let's apply this understanding about how memory works to forgetting. We now know that to remember anything for a long time, it must be transferred to long-term memory.

Many experiments on learning, and my own observations from over twenty-five years working with college students on study skills, point to the importance of *rehearsal*, or *review*, when you're learning new material.

There is simply no substitute for this important step.

In later chapters on reading and studying, we'll discuss several ways to rehearse new material to move it into long-term memory, but you now understand *why* this step is so important. *It takes advantage of how the brain is designed.*

The importance of such rehearsals in remembering new data is so significant and well-studied that psychologists can predict how much you'll forget (or remember) without (or with) the rehearsal step.

It can even be plotted on a graph, which is called *the Ebbinghaus Forgetting Curve.* For more theoretical (and practical) information, just search for "the forgetting curve."

If you don't rehearse new information—that is, if you go to class and listen to a lecture, for example, *and do nothing at all to review* *this new material—y*ou'll probably forget well over half of it in just one day!

But if you *do* review, studies suggest that you may recall as much as 80 percent of the new material—even after two months. *It's the review that "moves" this new* data into your long-term memory.

Or, to make a computer analogy, it's the review that "writes" new material to the hard-drive of your brain. If it doesn't get "written," it won't get saved.

Now Put This Information to Work Today!

So, now you know, in simplified form, how your memory works. New material first goes into short-term memory, which can easily be overloaded.

Your goal is to "move" this data into your long-term memory, and you do that by reviewing. Active reviewing is the way it's done.

Time is also important in this process, because research shows that *most forgetting happens in the first twenty-four hours*. If you don't review QUICKLY, you've missed the best opportunity to reinforce the new information and move it into your long-term memory.

So after class, if you can, go to the library (or a coffee shop) and read over your class notes—or discuss the lecture with a classmate. Go on a walk and talk to yourself about what you've just learned.

But try your best to do this initial review SOON after class for best results. *Reviewing can make the difference between forgetting 80 percent and remembering 80 percent of new material.*

And that is precisely what I mean by studying smarter, not harder.

Immediate review of new material is likely the most efficient thing you can do to learn better—and save study time, too.

As you'll learn in later chapters, this information about how memory actually works is the foundation for effectively reading, studying, and preparing for tests.

Review, and try to do it soon after you first receive the new information.

That's the key.

A Real-Life Example of How This Works

Here's an example of how effective this strategy can be from my own experience.

Raye, a freshman who was having trouble with the transition to college-level work, discovered first-hand how much this kind of immediate, elaborative rehearsal helped her in a difficult history class.

In the first half of the course, she struggled to pass tests (even though she had made terrific grades in high school). Her history professor was harder than any teacher she'd ever had, and there was more material to cover. She felt overwhelmed.

Thus, she was disappointed by her mid-term grades.

In the second half of the term, then, she decided that *she had to do something different* to improve her grades.

She made *one* crucial change in how she studied. After each lecture, she went straight to her dorm room and typed up the day's lecture notes, *adding in information she recalled but hadn't gotten down in her written class notes.*

Raye had figured out on her own how to improve her grades by typing her notes after class. Of course, she didn't know what you've just learned about the importance of immediate rehearsal, but she knew she had to do *something to raise her history grade.*

And it worked! she raised her test grades from a D to an A even though *she actually spent less time studying.* She didn't know *why* this new habit worked, but she was happy that it made such a difference in what she was able to remember.

Here's Why Raye's Study Changes Worked So Well

Now, in light of what we know about how memory actually works, notice what Raye accomplished by this one, simple, daily act:

1. After class she *immediately* typed her notes. At this point, her memory for the lecture was the best it would ever be, and she took advantage of that by not waiting till later in the day, or the weekend, to type up her notes. She didn't let anything else—conversations, TV, texting, or even other assignments—interfere with her memory of the class lecture.

2. By typing the lecture notes, she was *reviewing* what she had just learned. This *repetition* gave her brain another opportunity to further *consolidate* new information into long-term memory.

And the process of typing the notes gave her brain the *time* it needed to absorb the lecture.

3. By *adding* to what she had in her class notes, she was engaging in *elaborative rehearsal* (as we discussed earlier) which is a better way to transfer information to long-term memory than rote repetition.

4. By creating a *clear, concise set of typed notes*, she made it efficient to review just before the exam, which gave her *one more repetition* to strengthen her memory of the new information from this difficult history class.

Did Raye know how memory worked? Had she read the latest research on short-term and long-term memory?

No, she didn't know anything about the underlying explanation for why her study method was so effective. But, accidentally, she had stumbled on exactly the right form of effective study—*immediate repetition and enhanced "elaborative" rehearsal.*

She didn't know why her method worked, but now you do. And now you can apply the same strategies of repetition to make your own study time more effective and efficient.

PART THREE: ACADEMIC SKILLS

How to Take Great Notes in Class

The PART Reading System—How to Learn More in Less Time

The BEST Way to Study

Build A Powerful Memory

How to Be Testwise

How to Manage Test Anxiety

Chapter 10

How to Take Great Notes in Class

Now we're moving from general *support* skills to the specific *academic* skills you'll use each day in college.

Taking notes is an important academic skill because in college many professors use lectures to add to what's in the textbooks and other assigned readings.

That is, your instructors may simply assume that you'll master what's in the textbook on your on, so their lectures are intended to augment, discuss, explain, and go beyond the book.

Thus, your notes will be important.

You may not have needed to take notes in high school. Perhaps your tests came only from textbook material or study-sheets. Or maybe you could easily remember what the teachers said without taking complete notes.

It's a different situation in college.

To make good grades now, you need an accurate record of what your professors say in their lectures. Having good notes is the best way you can review what happens in class.

And, as the forgetting curve (discussed in the previous chapter) shows, *such reviews enable you to retain much more new information.*

Without good notes, what will you review?

What's more, taking good notes is important for another reason: *just the act of writing notes in class is a first rehearsal step*. You're going over the information as you write, and this is already helping transfer the new material to your long-term memory.

So taking notes is, itself, a way to learn new material.

Here's How to Take Effective Notes

As you take notes, these six techniques will help you record and learn *what's important* from each class.

1. *Use your binder to keep all your notes together.* Use dividers to organize your classes, and get a hole-punch so you can insert handouts, class schedules, and study sheets into the notebook where they belong.

2. *Don't try to take dictation when you take notes.* You can't, since professors talk much more quickly than you can write. (They probably speak 150-200 words a minute, while most people can only write about 25 words a minute. That's a huge difference.)

So how do you cope? What do you write?

First, *there is no need to write non-essential words* like *a, the*, and *an*. You want to get the *gist* of a comment, not a verbatim transcript. So just ignore those articles.

Next, since you can't write everything down, learn to concentrate on the important points.

But ... *how do you identify the important parts of a lecture?*

How to Know What's Important

First, *listen at the beginning of class for the day's topic*. The professor may be using an outline or notes for the lecture, and it is very likely to be an organized presentation. (Of course, that's not always true. Some professors may not be very organized so you'll have to listen especially carefully for their main points.)

Listen for repeated information. Watch carefully what's written on the board or included in a Power Point presentation.

Verbal cues are sometimes obvious, such as "To sum up, then," or "To repeat the point," or even "Now, the main point here is ..."

3. *Leave a wide margin along the left side* of each page of notes. About 2 inches is good. Leave this column blank at first. Later, you'll go back and add questions, or new information, in this space.

Creating questions as you study (an active-study method) is a technique that we'll discuss in depth later. For now, get in the habit of leaving a wide column on each page for the study questions and extra material you'll add.

You'll notice that many textbooks use a wide margin, both because white space is good design, and so that pertinent questions and observations printed there can point to relevant sections of the main text. You'll do the same with your class notes.

Book designers know the value of white space on a page for making things stand out. You can use the same approach, so don't crowd your notes on the page.

4. *Use a modified outline* as you take notes. Don't worry with formal outline formats, but just write a topic and indent supporting details under it. Write separate details on separate lines to make the details clearer. Don't write in paragraph format—*your goal is clarity when you take notes.*

You may have learned an orderly, coherent, proper outline technique, but when you're scrambling to take notes in class, you don't need to be particularly concerned about using correct form.

Let's say you're in my class where study skills are being taught. Here's how your notes from such a lecture might look:

Ideas for Taking Good Notes in Class

Use modified outline, like this:

—indent supporting details

—separate points on separate lines

—don't worry about letters, numbers for outline form

—use indents to organize/list under main point

—leave xtra white space

—don't fill page w/ notes

—leave wide margin/col on left to add info, questions later

That's the way it's done. It's possible, of course, that you'll be using a laptop, but most note-taking in class is still handwritten and this is still usually the quickest way to take notes. Plus, you'll find that the list format is much easier to study than long paragraphs.

Just be sure that you can read what you have written. There's no point in scribbling so fast that that you can't interpret your notes later when you need them!

5. *Leave lots of white space* in your notes. As mentioned above, you'll leave wide margins along the side for later questions, but you'll also come back later to add more information. You'll need space to add this new material.

An extra advantage is that lots of white space makes your notes much more readable. Of course you can always interpret your handwriting on the same day you write the class notes, but in three weeks you'll be glad you didn't try to cram too much on a page.

(Don't worry about wasting paper. It's cheap and paper is made from trees that are raised as a crop—not from old-growth forests. You can buy recycled paper, too. So, don't skimp.)

6. *Develop your own system of abbreviations.* You probably already use **&** or **+** instead of the word *and,* and of course you use lots of abbreviations when you text.

Now you'll add many more.

Here's a short list of typical abbreviations to get you started. Soon you'll begin to add many more that match your own interests, or specific terms that are repeated in your classes.

These shortcuts will become an automatic part of your own *Personal Learning System.* If you need to, make a list or legend so you won't forget what a new abbreviation means as you add it to your note taking.

w/ (with)

w/o (without)

c. (about, used w/ dates and number. Thus "c. 595" means "about 595.")

eg or ex (for example)

ie (that is, explanation)

b. (born)

d. (died)

(number)

#/ (number of)

gov't (government)

env (environment)

etc (and so forth)

re (regarding)

A related technique for taking notes is to simply omit vowels and silent letters. Thus:

sh (should)

wd (would)

cd (could)

Many people underline the last letter of an abbreviation to indicate the suffix "tion" and use a hyphen to indicate "ing." Thus "a<u>c</u>" means "action" and "act-" means "acting."

So, use what you already know from texting and add more useful personal shorthand expressions. Use these in class, and you'll save a lot of time taking notes.

You'll devise many abbreviations and note-taking shortcuts for yourself. When you find a word repeated often in your notes, develop a short way to write it. You'll save time and take better notes, too.

Just b sur u cn intrpt wht u wrt.

Note-Taking Review

Based on what you now understand about how the brain works, you are ready to make the best use of your class notes.

Review those notes the same day you take them. Remember the forgetting curve discussed earlier? If you *review* your notes very soon after taking them, you'll remember much more, and you won't need to re-learn everything when you study for exams.

Make this a rule that you use every day: **Review your notes the very same day you take them.** Remember Dr. Medina's term, *elaborative rehearsal* (described in chapter nine), and add new material as you go over the information you are learning.

Thus, as you review, add extra information that you couldn't get down during class. And write questions along the side, too. Later, we'll discuss the value of questions in more detail.

Taking good notes in class is a very important college skill and it takes practice. So remember these tips next time your professor is talking a mile a minute and you are scrambling to get it all down.

1. Learn to pick out the *main points*, and write them down first. You can add supporting details in an informal outline form, maybe just indenting supporting points under the main topic.

2. *Leave space along the side* to add more details later, and leave space for questions you may add as you study.

3. *Devise your own set of abbreviations* and shortened words. This will change and develop with different classes. Of course, an advanced biology class will have a different vocabulary from a modern European history course.

4. *Review your notes* the same day you take them. You'll be really surprised at how little time it takes to review your notes the same day.

And using this review strategy will save you an enormous amount of time when you're studying for exams because you will have remembered more.

5. This is so important I'll repeat it again for extra emphasis: ***review your notes the day you take them.***

Don't get discouraged if you don't feel that your notes are good in the beginning. It takes practice, and you'll get much better as you spend more time in college classes.

PLS Action Step 8

This is a two-part *PLS* step:

First, make your own list of useful abbreviations. Keep this list in your *PLS* notebook, and add new ones to it as you discover (or invent) them.

Be sure to create your own list of abbreviations. Don't just think about it or read over the list in this book or on the web. Why? Because *the very act of writing the list* helps you transfer this new information to your permanent memory—and that's where it belongs.

Next, practice these abbreviations as you take notes. The more you use them, the more automatic they will become, and the easier (and better) your note-taking will be.

Next, practice taking notes, using an informative TV show as your lecture. Perhaps the *History* or *Discovery* channel or PBS will have an interesting documentary tonight. Watch, listen, and pretend that it's a class lecture (but realize that professors typically talk much faster than commentators on TV, and a typical class lecture will have much more content than a TV show).

As you take notes, remember that *you're not trying to take dictation*. You simply can't do that.

Instead, *listen* for the main ideas, and put supporting information below those topic sentences.

Use a different line for each supporting point and *leave space* to come back and add more.

Use as much paper as you need, and *keep those notes* in an organized, easy-to-find place--your binder as the logical choice

Chapter 11

The PART Reading System—How to Learn More in Less Time

Think back to the last time you read a chapter in a textbook.

Did you remember what you had read by the next day's class? Maybe you even read it a second time . . . but still had trouble recalling the new information you were trying to learn.

Or, worse—have you spent time reading a difficult passage, and suddenly realized that you had *no idea what you'd just read*? That's disconcerting, and it is a big waste of your time.

You're going to have so much reading to do in college, most of it new material and much of it difficult, that it will pay you to spend some time learning *how to read effectively*.

"But," you may say, "I already know how to read. I've known since the first grade."

Wait! Don't skip this chapter because you may be surprised.

Most People Can REALLY Improve Their Reading With a Little Work

Unfortunately, most students learn to read early in school and don't get any instruction in reading techniques in later grades.

But the difficulty and sheer volume of what you're expected to read just goes up and up!

Further, today we live in such a high-speed digital culture that many students have never spent enough time reading books for it to be an easy, automatic, or pleasant experience.

All college students *can* read, of course, but many don't enjoy it . . . and aren't very good at it because no one has shown them how to improve.

Now that you're in college, the truth is that mediocre reading ability won't be good enough.

If you know that you already have trouble reading, you'll do much better in college if you can improve this vital skill before you start classes.

(And, if you have serious trouble reading, many colleges have reading labs with experts who can work with you and assess your particular problems.)

What's more, if you are an average or good reader, you'll still find that the techniques we discuss in this chapter will make you an even better, more efficient, reader.

What is Reading, Really?

Reading, physically, is moving your eyes along a line of text while your brain decodes the meaning. That's what you want to happen. You *want* your brain to take in the meaning of the words—and remember it.

But many students don't really complete the process of reading. Instead, they assume that if they've simply *run their eyes over a printed line*, they've read the material.

This, as you certainly know, really isn't *reading*. Reading a textbook, or chapter, or paper, means that you have *understood* that new material.

Understanding and remembering are really what you're after as you read. So, running your eyes over the printed page is important, but it's only part of the process.

The fact is that getting the most from reading, and remembering it, requires a lot of ability. You'll have thousands of pages to read as you go through college and you can't afford to approach this daunting task with inferior skills.

It's Not Getting Any Easier

Students today face a new kind of reading problem that their parents didn't confront.

Computers and other digital devices encourage *skimming* rather than the kind of attentive, focused reading that college requires. You know that you typically fly through emails, often skipping over long paragraphs. (Thus, many people have learned that emails must be short if they are to be read).

If you found an earlier edition of this book, you'd notice that the paragraphs are much shorter now. We made that change to match the way people read today because we know that long paragraphs often don't get read.

But *college reading is different from email or web surfing*. With college assignments, you can't skim. You must read closely to understand these long, detailed paragraphs and chapters.

In fact, what's required now is an entirely different *kind* of reading from what many students are used to.

When you study, you'll read for details, of course, but you'll also have to read for the big picture and not get lost in a mass of specific information. In fact, one of the students we interviewed in chapter 17, Elizabeth, makes this very point.

If you have problems reading and remembering, what can you do?

Simply reading a chapter over and over might be your first answer, but you won't have time for that approach.

And honestly, just rereading and rereading isn't very effective, anyway.

The answer is to use an *active, systematic approach to reading*.

Here's How to Read Better

The strategy I've developed from years of working with college students is called the **PART reading system**. When you use it, your reading comprehension can improve dramatically. You'll spend less time reading, won't have to constantly re-read, and you'll remember more.

Let me repeat that. When you use this system, you'll spend LESS time studying, and you'll remember MORE.

I call this a *system* partly to make it easy to remember, but once you understand the parts and start using them, it will be your natural approach. You won't just grab a new book and plunge right in, but you'll follow this plan. When you do, you'll find that *you get much more from your reading time*.

The four components of this approach to reading are:

1. **P**review

2. **A**ctively Read

3. **R**ehearse

4. **T**est Yourself

"P" is for *Preview*

Before you begin reading a new chapter or book, quickly scan through the pages to preview it and *get an overview of what you're about to learn.* It takes very little time but can dramatically increase your retention.

However, at first this *preview* step often seems a bit confusing. In workshops, students sometimes say, "Wait! This system is going to make me spend *more* time reading? I don't have any more time!"

In truth, if you follow this approach, you'll spend a lot *less* time reading overall because you'll be much more efficient. You won't constantly need to re-read and re-read again.

Spend a little more time in the beginning with this PREVIEW step, and you'll save a lot of time in the end. So, the first thing you're going to do is take the new book or chapter and *preview it* just as we did in the second chapter when we *previewed* this book.

Here's What to Preview

Thus, before you plunge into the body of the book, look over what you're about to read, and pay special attention to these six parts:

1. *Table of Contents*. Here, you'll get a quick glimpse at what's covered in the chapters to come. It's like a map you'd consult before starting out on a trip. In fact, that is a good comparison because a book is like a trip into unknown territory.

The table of contents will give you a general overview of where you are going, and it will be very helpful to have this big picture in mind as you proceed through the book.

As you *preview* the material, you'll also begin to think about the content, and you might even formulate some questions that you'll try to answer at the end.

2. *Arrangement of the chapter itself.* Look at the title, subtitles, headings, and summary within the chapter. The title and headings are like a mini-outline of a chapter. As you read them, think about where the chapter is going and what you'll be learning.

(For example, look at the subheading above. It tells you exactly what to expect as you read on in the chapter.)

As you preview further, keep the subheadings in mind as a kind of big "topic sentences" that illuminate the supporting material you're reading.

3. *Sidebars, pull quotes, and annotations* in the margins. These are design and typographic devices that add visual interest and emphasis to particular points.

Sidebars are like mini-articles within a chapter. They are often boxed or shaded to make them stand out and they typically amplify or expand on a topic that is mentioned in the main body of text.

These elements are included to make reading easier and to emphasize key points. Don't ignore them; they're there for a reason.

4. *Graphic elements.* These include photos, drawings, diagrams, maps, charts and graphs. These design items are more expensive to produce than text, so they are only included to call attention to the most essential ideas. Use them as clues to what's most important.

For example, a photo in a book about the building of the Panama Canal, for example, will really be worth a thousand words in setting the scene, or showing the construction machinery in action, or illustrating the attire and demeanor of the workers.

Often photos add much to your understanding and will give you a real preview of what you're about to read. *Don't ignore the captions because they are often very concise summaries of significant ideas.*

And maps will literally show you where in the world an event took place—they give crucial context and are exceptionally useful. *Maps are very helpful in understanding the big picture.*

5. *Questions at the end of a section* or in the margin help you focus on what you're about to learn, so read them quickly as you preview. Asking questions is a powerful way to learn and *a quick glance at end-of-chapter questions will tell you what to look for as you read.*

This is a very useful preview strategy.

6. *Summary.* If the chapter has a summary at the end, read it FIRST.

It will highlight the main concepts of the chapter and really help you keep the big picture in mind. Maybe it seems odd to read the end (summary) of a chapter first (as you preview), but it's a very helpful technique.

Now, this kind of preview really only takes a couple of minutes. But here's what you've gotten in that short time.

* You now have a clear idea of *where* the chapter is going.

* You know *what* you'll be covering.

* You know how much space is allotted to different topics, and that tells you *what's important in the text.*

And now you know that end-of-chapter questions are like the author and editors taking you by the hand to point out *exactly what's most important* in what you've just read.

Don't think that you can skip or skimp on this step. Before you start out on any reading journey, spend a few minutes with the map—the preview—so you have a general idea of where the reading will take you.

You'll be amazed at how this helps you focus and maintain concentration and perspective.

And, here's the surprising advantage of doing a preview: *it actually saves time.* After a preview, you'll read the chapter in *less time* than it would take if you'd just forged ahead with no idea of where you were going.

Now, since you'll have an idea of what you're about to learn, your mind will be more active as you read the author's supporting points and arguments.

So that's the first step in the PRT approach to reading—PREVIEW. Don't just plunge in to reading a chapter but take a few moments to *preview* what you're about to learn.

PLS Action Step 9

Using a textbook, *preview* the next chapter you'll be studying just as described above. Look at the chapter title, subtitles, pull quotes, sidebars, photos, photo captions, maps, and other graphic elements, and glance over any questions at the end.

Time yourself as you preview this chapter. You'll be amazed at how much you'll learn from this simple step, and at how little time it takes.

Your goal is to make *previewing* a normal, everyday, habitual part of your reading. Spend a little time on this step, and you'll be amazed at how it helps you get more from your reading and study time.

"A" Is for *Actively Read*

You've just done the first step of the **PART** system, and have *previewed* a chapter (or book) so you have a sense of where you're about to go. Now it's time to actually read the chapter.

Since the preview has shown the general, broad outline, you'll now look for details and supporting facts.

As you read, remember that the key word for this step (and other study tips throughout this book) is *active*. Stop trying to read if your attention begins to drift, or you find yourself daydreaming, or you feel that you simply must check Facebook and all the rest.

With the **PART** reading system, you're not just going through the motions anymore; you're *actively reading*, looking for answers and support for the ideas you got from the preview. You simply can't do it if your mind is somewhere else.

Here are five tips to help you stay active as you read:

1. *Use those subtitles and headings* to understand a specific purpose for reading *each* section. If a subhead says, "Socrates' Trial," then you'll know you're about to learn details about this event.

So, in this example, you'll want to know *what* it was, *why* it was held, *who* the participants were, *the charges* against Socrates, something about *the Greek judicial system* and *the outcome*.

That is, *from the subhead, you now know what you're about to learn* and your interest is stimulated.

You'll be a better reader because you're now looking *actively* for those details about Socrates' trial.

Use the subheads, then, in everything you read. They'll guide you through the chapter, and help keep your mind active.

2. Pay special attention to the *main points*. They'll often be at the beginning of a paragraph or section. Further, they will often be in **bold**, or *italic* type, and they may be repeated, or summarized, at the end of a section.

Sometimes, the main points are summarized or condensed as pull quotes in the margin, or set in a box to make them stand out from the rest of the text.

Use these cues to find out what's most important as you read. When you are reading a lot of new material, it is very helpful to be able to know what the main points are so you won't get lost in the details.

On an exam, there will surely be times when you can't recall all the supporting facts that you'd like to use, *but if you have a good grasp of the main points, you'll often do surprisingly well.*

3. Now, as you read, look for the *supporting facts and arguments*. They'll follow the main point. The body of a paragraph usually explains and provides details. If you keep the *purpose* of the paragraph in mind, you won't get lost in all that material.

4. *Ask yourself questions* as you read. Look for the answers. Or, pretend to have a conversation (or even an argument) with the author.

Questions such as, "Why does he say that?" or "Why is this important?" can really help keep your mind engaged and should become a routine part of your reading.

5. *Be careful that your mind doesn't drift* away while you are reading. This is a danger all the time, of course, because there is a lot going on in your life, but you'll learn better, and ultimately spend

less time reading and studying if you can keep your focus on the task at hand.

If you feel your attention weakening, take a 10-minute break and try again.

Ultimately, *reading is a waste of time if you're not focused on what you are doing,* and in college you don't have time to waste.

In some ways, the term *reading* is itself misleading, because what you're really doing is *thinking.* It's true that you are moving your eyes along lines of type, but *the real process takes place inside your actively engaged mind.*

PLS Action Step 10

Using an assigned chapter in a textbook, practice the first two steps of the **PART** system.

First, *preview the chapter* as discussed above.

Then, *actively read* it.

Look first for the *main points.* Then note the *supporting data.*

Ask yourself questions as you read, using titles and subheads as guides, and be sure your attention stays focused.

When you finish the chapter, compare what you've learned with your old way of reading, and *decide to make active reading a habit.*

"R" Is for *Rehearse*

Rehearse means to review, practice, or go back over the material you're learning.

This is the MOST IMPORTANT step you can take to remember what you've read.

Why is this true? Think back to our discussion of how memory works, and the "forgetting curve." To *transfer* information from short- to long-term memory we must review (or *rehearse*) the material or we will forget it.

And as we *rehearse* new material, we help that crucial transfer to take place. There are really two kinds of rehearsal described in this book:

1. When you study, *you'll rehearse the material you're learning by self-testing*. I'll describe this powerful way to prepare for exams in the next chapter.

2. The *rehearse* step in the **PART** system, however, is different.

Now, we are talking about the rehearsal and *immediate review that you will do as you read.* It includes not only stopping to think about what you're learning, but also taking notes as you go along.

As you read, then, stop frequently to go over, in your mind or on paper (or on your laptop), what you're learning.

Think again about the image of a quart jar overflowing when you pour too much water into it. That's how your brain reacts to too much information coming at it without pause.

So stop to think about what you're reading. That will give your brain a chance to process this new information. As current research shows, that processing time is very important.

Is there a best way to rehearse? In fact, there are at least three different ways to review new material as you read: *visual, auditory*, and *hands-on*. Different people prefer different styles, and these different approaches don't all work the same for everyone, so use the one that is most effective for you.

Visual Learners

Many students are *visual learners* and learn most quickly by taking notes over what they read. If this is your style, here are five techniques for taking notes so you can rehearse effectively.

In other words, visual learners will rehearse best by writing down, and *seeing,* the new material.

1. *Flash cards* help many students take notes on their reading. Buy a stack of index cards and write a question on one side. Put the answer, including facts and details, on the other.

2. When possible, *include specific numbers* in notes or questions. Specific numbers help you remember—they're like hooks. Some visual learners may even remember how the figures look on the page.

For example, your card might have the question, "Name 3 solid parts of the blood." You would then write the answer on the back of your card, and the very act of making up the question (active learning) and writing the question and answer (visual learning) is helping your brain *rehearse* this new material and move it into long-term memory.

3. Take notes only over the most important facts. *Don't simply recopy the text.* Use the note-taking techniques discussed earlier.

You may be wondering, "Can't I just highlight the important points with a yellow marker? That seems *very* visual!"

Lots of students do make extensive use of yellow, blue, and pink highlighters but it's usually not the most effective way to study.

You may actually highlight too much because *if you emphasize everything, you're really emphasizing nothing.* Many students don't really understand this advice at first, and if you'd like to see more about it, just Google "over-highlighting and study."

There is the danger, too, that highlighting gives the illusion that you're actively thinking about what you're reading—but your mind isn't really actively engaged.

It's much better to take notes. If you do underline or highlight, just mark a few carefully selected points. Don't overdo it.

4. Make the most important points *visually stand out* as you take notes. Many visual learners will actually remember how a page looks, so use white space, separate lines, stars, and underlining— and diagrams and simple drawings—to make important points leap off the page at you.

5. If you prefer notebook paper to cards for note-taking, it's useful to draw a vertical line to divide the page. Leave a two-inch margin on the left for study questions you'll add later. *Take your notes on the right side of the page.*

And, if you're using a computer, a simple table with two columns is one quick and easy way to set up this question/answer note-taking method. Questions go in the left column, and your notes and answers should be on the right.

Auditory Learners

Other students are *auditory learners*, and learn best by *hearing* new information. If you learn most efficiently this way, here are three tips to use as you actively rehearse what you're reading.

1. *Talk about what you've just read.* Perhaps you can explain the material to a study partner. Or, you can talk to yourself, either out loud or silently. (If you're wearing a Bluetooth earpiece or earplugs, no one will think twice if you're walking around campus talking to yourself. They won't even know you're studying!)

2. Some auditory learners use small recorders as their note-taking medium. Small digital recorders are handy for this purpose, especially the devices that record to SD cards for easy file transfer. Or you can use the recorder function in your phone, of course.

For these students, it's effective to read part of a chapter, and then dictate their notes. When they do, *the act of speaking helps them remember*; it's a kind of rehearsal.

Of course, with this method, you can also listen to your notes when you study and as you walk or commute to class (and re-listening to a lecture can be very helpful).

3. Another excellent way for auditory learners to rehearse as they read is to *teach* the new material to someone. You can actually teach a classmate or study partner, or just pretend, by talking to yourself as if you were explaining the new material. Some students find it handy to set up a whiteboard at home, and write on it as if they were teaching a class.

If you can teach it, you're very likely to know it.

Hands-on Learners

A third learning style is that of the *hands-on learner*. These tactile learners may rehearse new material by creating a model of what they're learning.

They might draw a diagram, for example, or actually build a replica or representation of the subject. This learning style is less common than the first two, but if you learn best by doing, look for ways to incorporate hands-on action into your rehearsal step.

Of course, many people combine elements of all three learning styles, so as you rehearse what you've read, use the method, or combination of methods, that seems most effective to you.

Whether you take notes on paper or cards, use a digital recorder, or build a model, the active *rehearse* step is very important to successful reading. Why? Because going over the new material gives the brain time to transfer it to your long-term memory.

And, of course, rehearsal is an active step that keeps your attention focused on what you're doing.

"T" Is for *TEST*

The final step of the **PART** reading system makes sure that you know what you've read and helps you prepare for exams.

This step, testing yourself, is a very powerful study technique. In fact, it's such a good way to prepare for tests that if you really use it, you'll likely see your grades go up immediately. And if that happens it's proof that you really are learning.

So whether you're just finishing a chapter for a daily reading assignment, or studying it for a final exam, use this technique.

Here's how to test yourself as you read:

1. *Get the big picture first.* Be sure you understand the main points. That way, you'll understand how the supporting facts fit together. So, start by testing yourself on the big picture, the broad outlines of the subject.

Do you need help identifying what's most important? Clues to recognizing the main points include chapter titles, headings, and first sentences in paragraphs.

Here's an easy, active, and effective technique for testing yourself as you read: *reword chapter titles and subheadings into questions.*

Thus, if the chapter title is, "Whitman's Use of Poetic Devices," your quick rewording would be something like, "Describe Whitman's use of poetic devices." This technique helps you focus immediately on what's most important.

Always ask: *What is the main point of this chapter?* Have this clearly in mind before you start reading and studying supporting details.

2. *Make up realistic, tough questions* on your reading. Don't cheat yourself by making them easy, because your professors' questions will be difficult.

In fact, this final step of the **PART** reading system—testing yourself —is one of the best approaches to all kinds of study, because it is *active*, and it forces you to understand the material. The big difference between self-testing and your professor's exams, obviously, is that when you're testing yourself, you will go back and immediately review what you don't know.

Are you having trouble making up good questions for testing yourself?

Then use the journalistic technique of "Five W's and an H." That is, ask *Who, What, Where, When, Why* and *How* about the new material.

If you can answer these questions about what you're reading, you've learned it.

Adapting the PART System to Math Classes

The principles that form the **PART** reading system can also be used for math classes. So, when you are studying math, use the same four steps:

Preview the chapter, or heading, by reading the explanatory material.

Actively tackle the problems. Actually work—that is, don't just look at (or think about) the sample problems. Math is definitely a field where you learn by doing.

Then work through the problems in each section. Typically, math problems are arranged in order of difficulty. As you work the problems, compare your answers to those provided by the professor or in the back of your textbook.

Rehearse/Review regularly. In math, this can be fairly easy. Each day before you start on a new section or new problems, go back and *rework* three (or more) problems from those you did the day before. Choose one easy problem, one that's moderately hard, and one that's difficult.

Reworking those problems will keep your memory of this information strong, and will assure that your mind is fully in gear before you tackle new material.

Test yourself. Be sure to test yourself the same way that your professor will test you. In chapter 12, we'll describe how one highly-motivated pre-med student raised his grade in a math class by creating (and taking) his own tests. It's a very, very effective study technique.

Learning Through Testing—What the Research Says

In an interesting study at Purdue University, a large group of college students was divided into four sub-groups. Each group read a short science article on a subject such as "The Digestive Tract." One week later they were tested to see how much they recalled from the article.

Group 1 simply read the article in five minutes. Group 2 studied the passage in 4 consecutive 5-minute sessions, which is similar to cramming for a test.

Group 3 created a "concept map" with the test passage in front of them. They wrote details from the article in a kind of diagram with interconnected lines.

Group 4 (called the "retrieval practice group") read the article, then *without* the passage in front of them, they wrote a short summary of it from memory. (This is what we call the *rehearsal step* in the **PART** system.) Then this group re-read the article and took a short test over the material.

One week later all students were tested. Researchers found that those in Group 4, (the "retrieval practice group"), scored significantly higher than subjects in the other groups.

The scientists concluded that the process of having to retrieve the information from memory by summarizing it, and then taking a test over the material, was far more effective than other methods.

In fact, students using this "retrieval method" (which is very similar to the *Rehearse* and *Test* steps that you are learning in this chapter) recalled about 50 percent more of the information a week later than those using other methods.

So, when you want to remember what you have read, use the **PART** system, and you'll be happily surprised at your results.

PLS Action Step 12

Write ten good questions on a chapter you're studying now.

If you've taken notes on notebook paper, you should have a two-inch column down the left side of each page as described earlier. Now, write your questions there, next to related information.

If you're using a laptop, devise a way to write questions while leaving plenty of room for answers. Some students just make a list of questions, while others may use a table—but in any case leave enough space for answers.

And if you're using note-cards, write questions on one side and answers on the back.

PLS Action Step 13

Now, try the complete **PART** reading system on a chapter you're assigned to study.. This is the best way to understand how easy and natural it is to use this approach to reading.

At first it make take you longer to use each of the four steps, but soon you'll be learning more in less time (which is our goal).

Remember to use each part of our reading strategy because they work together.

To review, *the PART Reading System* means that you'll:

Preview,

Actively Read,

Rehearse, and

Test yourself

You'll see how this approach to reading works as you go through each step. And, when you realize how much more you remember from your reading and study, *you'll begin to use this approach all the time.*

Chapter 12

How to Study The BEST Way

Now you're taking good notes in class and as you study, you're using the **PART** system when you read. Plus, you now understand the importance of rehearsing new material because you know how your memory works.

So, you've just looked at the class syllabus –and next week you have a major exam.

What study techniques will make the best use of your time and energy?

Are some study methods better than others?

Or is it best to grit your teeth and plan on a couple of late-night cram sessions as the test date approaches?

There's no need to just plow ahead as you study. Simply spending more time staring at a book is not the answer.

In fact, smart students use a rifle (rather than a shotgun) approach to learning new material because it saves a lot of time.

Target Your Study Time

Here are two effective techniques to *focus your study efforts most effectively*.

1. If you used notebook paper to take notes on your reading, you should have a wide column for questions along the left side of each page. Write questions now, if you haven't already, over the material in your notes.

As you study, cover the right side of the page, and ask yourself the questions from the left column. When you get one right, go on to the next question.

If you don't feel confident about an answer, *mark that spot on the page with a paper clip*. Then, return to it later. Don't remove the paper clip until you're sure you know the answer.

And sometimes it's most effective to come back to the difficult questions later, rather than just going over and over and over complicated new material.

This way, a simple paper clip becomes a powerful study tool, because it reminds you of *exactly* what you need to review. It helps you focus specifically on *what is yet to be learned*.

2. If you used index cards to take notes during the review step of the **PART** reading system, then you'll use them now to study. As you did your reading, you wrote questions on one side of each card and the answers on the back.

Now, ask yourself the questions from the front of the cards. If you get the answer right, put the card to your left. If your answer is incomplete, put it to your right.

Then, *review only the cards on your right* until you're satisfied that you really know the answers to each question.

Why This Study System Works So Well

There are many advantages of studying by *self-testing* this way.

First, the simple question-and-answer technique is an *active* form of study. Your mind will be in gear as you work. If you're asking questions and answering them, then your mind isn't wandering.

You're focused, and that's the goal for active, effective studying.

Next, by going back over only the material you *don't* know, you'll save lots of time. Here's where the lowly paper-clip and index cards become highly effective study tools.

This, then, is the core of the very effective self-testing approach to studying: you zero in on what you don't yet know and *don't waste time going over and over everything.*

Ultimately, you'll feel more confident when you prepare this way for tests. After all, if you can answer the difficult questions that you ask yourself, you know you can answer similar questions on an exam!

Self-testing is a powerful way to study, but there is one more thing to think about. You must be sure that your questions are complete and that they really cover the topic you're learning.

Thus, as you test yourself, use class notes, textbooks, web resources, extra reading, and handouts to be sure you aren't overlooking important points.

Use the syllabus, too, to be sure you haven't skipped anything important. The professor didn't spend time creating the syllabus just for fun. You're supposed to follow it.

And, if the professor distributes an old exam for study, be sure you make use of it. Previous exams from a class give a strong indication of what new tests from that professor may be like.

However, *only rely on such old exams as a rough guide* to what you might see on current tests. It's useful, but it's *not* a guarantee that future exams will be similar.

How One Student Used Self-Testing in Math

John, a highly-motivated pre-med student I worked with, developed a very effective system of self-testing for a math class he was taking. He was doing fairly well in the class, mostly making B's on quizzes and tests, but he knew it was important for him to make A's since admission to a nationally-ranked medical school was his goal.

John analyzed what he was doing wrong and discovered that his biggest problem was that *he was working too slowly* on quizzes and tests.

Thus he often wasn't able to finish tests, and obviously this hurt his grades. It was frustrating, because he *knew* the material—he just didn't have time to complete the exams.

So here's what he did.

John decided to construct some practice tests to try to speed up his test-taking skills, so he created tests for himself that were as close as possible to the tests he expected his professor to give.

Then, as he studied, he wrote out sample problems (along with the directions for each type of problem). He made these quizzes and tests the same length he expected in class—for example, quizzes always had 10 problems.

John made three sample quizzes for himself every time he was to have a quiz in class.

Then, he timed himself. At first, he allowed himself exactly the same amount of time he would have in class—typically 30 minutes. That way, it was realistic and exactly like the real test environment.

But then, he made it harder. As he continued to study and prepare for an upcoming exam, he gave himself *less* time than he would have in class—first 28 minutes, then 25 minutes.

In other words, he gave himself three sample quizzes in preparation for the upcoming class quiz, *and his own practice tests were harder than the real quiz would be.*

As you might expect, John's plan worked beautifully. After developing this self-testing technique, he found that on his actual quizzes, he now had no trouble finishing in the 30 minute limit.

And John achieved his goal—an A in this math class.

Now Try This Yourself

If you're taking a math class, try John's self-testing technique for yourself. Create your own test, making it as much as possible like the one you expect from your professor. (Use problems for which you have the answers so you can check yourself.)

It's extremely important to write the directions for each type of problem, just the way they are written in your textbook—like "Solve for X"—because reading the instructions for each problem takes time during the exam.

Then time yourself. Take your own test. Check your answers and review any that you missed. If you find that you work too slowly, consider following John's strategy and create two or more of your own tests over the same material. Then time yourself again—and push to work faster.

By creating your own practice tests, you'll be thoroughly prepared to do well on any math test you take. And, like John, you'll be rewarded with higher grades.

Does it take time to study this way?

Of course it does, but college is your job, and your goal is to do well. If it takes time to reach that goal, it's time very well spent!

PLS Action Step 14

Here's an experiment that can pay off immediately with better grades. For your next exam, study using *self-testing* as described above.

Use notebook paper or cards, and *write* as many relevant questions as you need to feel confident about the subject. (Be sure you can answer the questions, of course!). If you are studying for a math exam, devise your own practice tests, as John did.

Remember that *just thinking about the questions is not at all the same as actually writing them down.*

Some experts are convinced that writing on a computer is less effective than writing by hand, but we think the essential point is to take time to actually record your questions. *It's a physically active step in studying.*

(For more on research about handwriting, "brain training," and enhanced learning, search online for "How Handwriting Trains the Brain." It's fascinating—and may honestly help you learn faster.)

Now, if possible, have someone ask you the questions you've developed. This is where a study partner or group can be helpful. *Only return to those questions that you miss.*

If you're studying alone, use the paper clips to mark parts of the text (or your notes) that you need to review, or separate your note-cards into *know* and *don't know* stacks.

This is the rifle-shot approach that zeros in on areas that need the most work. Use it and save hours of studying, because you'll truly be working *smarter*—not *harder*.

Everyone has the same 24 hours in a day, but wise use of your study time will make studying and learning more efficient and effective.

Chapter 13

How to Build a Powerful Memory

You already know how your memory works and how to apply that knowledge to note-taking and reading.

That means that you now understand why *frequent reviews* are so important when you're learning anything. This isn't theory, but is well understood and well documented by brain research.

But, as you go through college, you have to remember much more than the main points in your textbooks.

You have to learn all kinds of specific facts, lists, figures, details, terms, formulas, dates, names, and specialized vocabularies. Sometimes you just absolutely have to memorize new material.

Frequently, you can learn facts in context, and this often helps. For example, if you're studying the Civil War, you might learn about the causes, strategy, personnel, and outcome of the Battle of Chickamauga.

For studying subjects such as history, where all the facts may be presented chronologically, approach the new material *as if it were a story*, with a beginning, middle, and end, and with a cast of characters. When there are many pieces that fit together coherently, it can help your understanding and memory *because it makes sense.*

Six Tips for Remembering Lists

Often, though, you'll simply have to memorize lists of unrelated material. Vocabulary for foreign languages, definitions for a science course, or technical terms for an accounting class are a few examples of topics that need to be memorized.

Fortunately, for these cases there are useful techniques and shortcuts that can make memorizing unrelated facts much easier.

The suggestions in this chapter will help you master such lists of new data. Of course, nothing can make it easy to memorize lists of difficult material, but these tips show you how to be as efficient as possible.

1. Use the *Rule of Seven* when you're learning lists. Group the items you're learning in sets of about seven, and you'll learn them much faster.

Phone numbers (without area codes) are seven digits, and zip codes are five digits. Your social security number and credit-card numbers are broken down into three- and four-digit segments for a reason.

It's much easier to remember that way.

Have you installed software lately? The installation key may be 20 digits or more, but it's usually presented in groups of four. That makes it more understandable and *much* easier to work with.

So, don't try to memorize a long string of new items at once. *Group them into chunks of about 7 units* and spread out your study time.

For instance, if you study the first seven items in a list early in the day, and the next seven in the afternoon, you'll learn them faster and more easily. This is a practical application of what we have learned about short-term memory—it works best if it's not overloaded.

2. Take advantage of the *First and Last Effect*. In learning a list, it's easier to remember the **first and last items** on the list.

So, use index cards for tackling lists of vocabulary words or new terms. Mix them up as you study. Sometimes go from last to first. Sometimes start in the middle.

Vary what's first and what's last because you'll learn the list more quickly (and more thoroughly) if you do.

(Musicians often use this technique in memorizing long pieces. Rather than always playing from the beginning, they vary the starting point when they practice. Consequently, they are able to learn the piece much more quickly—and more thoroughly.

Actors approach long scripts the same way. They learn a part thoroughly by NOT always starting at the beginning of a passage. Sometimes they start in the middle. Sometimes they study from a random point, which helps assure that they really know their parts.)

3. Use the *Power of Organization*. Group the items you're learning together in logical form. Try to find ways to link unrelated items or categorize them into sets.

Rather than struggling with learning all the countries in South America straight from a list, for example, you'd do better to organize the countries into groups. Make up categories or groups that make sense to you.

Here's an example of sample groupings you might devise:

Countries starting with A-M

Countries starting with N-Z

Countries on the equator

Countries above the equator

Countries below the equator

Countries with coastlines on the Atlantic, Caribbean, Pacific

Countries speaking Spanish

Countries speaking languages other than Spanish

Or, use any other grouping you wish. Imposing order of some sort will make learning lists like this much easier.

4. Use *Personal Associations* whenever you can. Your mind is already stocked with your life experiences, and if you can link new subjects with what you already know, learning will be quicker, and you'll likely remember more.

5. Use *Mnemonic Devices* (pronounced *knee MON ick*). These rhymes, sentences, songs, and made-up words have been used for centuries to help remember items in order. They can be complex or simple, and you can make them up as you need them.

In fact, it's surprising how effective this technique can be.

Often memory celebrities who regularly astound audiences with their stunning stage acts use some form of mnemonic devices. That's hot it's possible for these accomplished memory experts to remember so much information. You've probably seen such a performance in person or on TV.

Here are six well-known mnemonic devices. There are many more, and you can—and should—create more of your own.

■ *HOMES* cues students to recall the Great Lakes: Huron, Ontario, Michigan, Erie, and Superior. Remembering these five lakes is much, much easier when you simply remember the cue-word, *HOMES*.

That's how mnemonic devices work.

■ *Please Excuse My Dear Aunt Sally* reminds students of the order of operations in solving math equations (parentheses, exponents, multiplication, division, addition, subtraction). Somehow, remembering the mnemonic sentence, silly as it is, is easier than remembering the list of operations.

■ *Roy G. Biv* is another well-known mnemonic device that helps students remember the names and order of the colors of the spectrum: red, orange, yellow, green, blue, indigo, violet.

■ *Every Good Boy Does Fine,* and *All Cows Eat Grass* are traditional ways to remember the lines and spaces of the musical staff (E, G, B, D, F and A, C, E, G).

■ *My Very Eager Mother Just Served Us Nachos* is another made-up phrase that prompts students to recall the planets in order: Mercury, Venus, Earth, Mars, Jupiter, Saturn, Uranus, and Neptune. Somehow the meaningless phrase makes it easier to remember the planets and their order. Perhaps this is strange, and it may seem a bit silly, but it works!

■ *On Old Olympus' Towering Top, a Finn and German Viewed a Hop* is one of many mnemonic devices used by medical students to master all the information they must learn. This one is used to recall the names and order of the cranial nerves.

Want proof that these memory-aids work? Ask your doctors if they still remember them from medical school. Chances are, they will.

So, to remember random lists and new terms, *create your own mnemonic devices*. And, if you're interested, visit Wikipedia's mnemonics page, or just Google the term. You'll be amazed and amused, and you'll probably find several examples you can use.

To use this idea, create words, phrases, or even little rhymes, and they will really help you recall terms in order. If they are funny or absurd, you may remember them more easily.

6. Make up a song. This self-made mnemonic device can be very effective. You know how aggravating an ear-worm can be—a jingle or the hook from a song that won't leave your head, and now you can put this concept to productive use.

Here's a good example of the value of songs for memorizing new things. You probably learned the alphabet from that famous little "a, b, c" song. No doubt, you can sing it right now.

There is something about music that makes words much easier to remember, and there has been lots of scientific work on this idea. You can set a list of unrelated items to a melody that you already know, and if you sing it to yourself a few times, chances are that you'll remember it. Maybe forever.

For many examples in a variety of fields, search YouTube for "mnemonic songs." You'll find songs from the a-b-c's to the periodic tables to complex medical lingo. *These songs exist because they help people remember things.*

Try it yourself and see.

How Memory Experts Do It

Maybe you've seen people on TV who have absolutely prodigious memories—people who can memorize very, very long lists of unrelated names, or all the cards in a shuffled deck, in just a few minutes. There are international memory competitions, and the winners have nearly unbelievable memory skills, but they were not born with such outstanding memories.

Could you develop such a powerful memory? Would it be useful in your college life?

The answer may surprise you—it's likely that anyone can develop an outstanding memory by using the right method.

The techniques used by real memory experts usually involve a "memory mansion," which is a way of *attaching specific things you need to remember to items and places that you already know.*

It sounds odd and clumsy and you wouldn't think it could work— but almost all the real memory Olympians use some form of this technique.

A fascinating book about a normal guy who impulsively decides to enter an international memory contest is *Moonwalking with Einstein: The Art and Science of Remembering Everything*. It's an interesting story—your library probably has a copy. (And, while it's not intended as a 'how-to' manual, you'll learn precisely how memory experts do it and you'll pick up lots of useful tips.)

PLS Action Step 15

Here's a list of the first ten Presidents of the United States. Using the first initials of their names, make up a mnemonic device and see how much it helps you remember these names in order. Remember, your made-up device can be a word, phrase, poem, or sentence.

Or, you might decide to set these names to a song.

The names:

Washington

Adams

Jefferson

Madison

Monroe

Adams

Jackson

Van Buren

Harrison

Tyler

When you've created your mnemonic device from this list, use it to study the ten names, and see how much easier it makes such memorization tasks.

Chapter 14

How to Be Testwise

Everyone knows that tests aren't perfect. But, we also know that tests of some sort will always be with us. Even after you've graduated, you'll still be tested and evaluated. Rankings and ratings are an unavoidable part of life.

Next time you're in a bookstore or online, look at books on "Test Preparation." You'll see dozens (or hundreds) of study books for all kinds of specialized tests.

So, even if your college is one of the rare ones that doesn't give tests or you've been a home-schooler who didn't take them, a glance at shelf after shelf of test preparation books for both academic and vocational tests will convince you that *there are lots of exams in your future.*

Interestingly, you'll use the same test-taking techniques for all kinds of tests, even those you'll take years from now, so being test-wise will help you on the GRE and specialized graduate-school admissions tests like the GMAT (business school), the MCAT (medical school), and the LSAT (law school).

That's because when you're really test-wise, you'll practice many of the same approaches regardless of the tests' content.

If you use the note-taking, reading, and study methods presented in this book, you'll already be preparing for both teacher-made and standardized exams by learning the material well.

The Best Strategy of All: Be Prepared

Of course (and quite obviously), the first and most important principle of being test-wise is to *be prepared*. Know what you're supposed to know. Study wisely, and test yourself with realistic questions.

No test-taking strategy can compensate for lack of knowledge. The test-taking techniques in this chapter are not crutches; they won't substitute for good studying. And they shouldn't.

Your real goal in college is to learn as much as you can, and the goal of an exam is to measure your success.

However, despite all your good studying and preparation, you should still learn *how* to take the most common types of tests so you can be sure to show what you know.

The 33 test-taking techniques and tips in this chapter will help you do as well as possible on multiple-choice and essay exams. Are these methods important? Yes, they are. That's because just knowing *how* to take a test properly can raise your score a letter grade or more.

Seven Tips for Taking Multiple-Choice Tests

Some people think multiple-choice tests are easier than other formats because, after all, the answer is given. All you have to do is recognize it.

Don't be fooled. Even though the correct answer is right there in front of you as one of the choices, multiple-choice tests can be very, very difficult and tricky.

So, here are seven strategies that will help you with all kinds of multiple-choice exams.

1. *Read each question carefully and completely.* Don't jump to conclusions. It's easy to assume that you know what's being asked, but *every* word in *each* question (and in each answer) is important.

So, don't skim quickly over answers, and don't read only the first part of an answer and assume that you know what the rest of it says. Speed reading is a good skill to have—but not when you're taking an exam.

With multiple-choice tests, you must read carefully. Very carefully.

2. *Finish the exam in the allotted time.* Often, questions you don't answer are counted as wrong. Wear a watch and keep up with the time. Decide before you begin how much time each question should take.

Of course, there will be variations, but keep the big picture of your progress through the exam clearly in mind.

Being aware of the clock helps assure that you won't run out of time before you've been through all the questions.

One technique is to go through the exam twice. The first time, answer all the easy questions, the ones you immediately know.

Then, on the second pass, concentrate on the difficult questions that require more time. That way, you at least get to all the questions that you easily can answer.

Just be sure that you don't lose your place on the answer sheet. This is more important than it may sound for paper tests (though it's not an issue for computer-based exams). It only takes a fraction of a second to be sure the number of each question corresponds to where you are on the answer sheet. This is an easy habit to establish and can literally save an exam.

3. *Underline the key words in each question* (if you are allowed to write on the test). This forces you to *focus on what is being asked.*

If you're taking a computer-based exam, or can't write on the test itself, then *hear yourself read the question silently.* Put extra stress on the important words, and pay attention to the verbs in the question.

Be positive that you are clear about exactly what each question is asking, because the wording of the question may be (intentionally) tricky.

Underlining key words (or silently speaking the question to yourself with emphasis on those key words) will help you be sure you are answering exactly what is being asked.

4. *Read every answer.* Even if you think the first choice is correct, read them all. Often there is a good answer . . . and a better one. To repeat the first tip in this list, *never jump to conclusions.*

Read every word of every answer before you make your final choice.

Eliminate each answer that you know is wrong. Mark through it if you're allowed to write on the test. This reduces the amount of information you must hold in your short-term memory and makes the selection process easier.

6. *Read the question and the answer you've chosen together* to check for logical and grammatical consistency.

Think of the question as the *subject* of a sentence, and the answer as the *predicate*. Together, they should make sense. If there is an obvious grammatical mismatch in part of the question, for example, that answer is probably wrong.

7. Watch carefully for *absolutes* and *qualifiers*. These are clues that often help you decide whether an answer is correct. This can be an important cue as you think through the possible answers.

Absolutes are words that leave NO room for any exceptions, such as *always* and *never*. They often indicate an incorrect answer because so few situations are absolute.

Here's an example. Perhaps you are taking an exam in human biology, and one question is about the amount of blood in human bodies. If an answer says, "All adults have 5 liters of blood," the absolute word *all* is a strong clue that this is an incorrect choice. Common sense, as well as your studying, tells you that people of different sizes will have different amounts of blood.

So, always watch carefully for *absolute* words in answers. They often indicate a wrong answer.

Qualifiers, on the other hand, are words that do make room for exceptions. Examples include such words as *often* and *rarely*. Qualified answers are often correct.

(Notice that the preceding sentence, *qualified answers are often correct*, is itself qualified with the word *often*. Think about how different the meaning would be had we written, "Qualified answers are *always* correct.")

Let's rephrase the example used above from the human biology class. If a possible answer had been, "An average adult has about 5 liters of blood," it's easy to see how different the meaning is from the absolute version above. The qualifiers *average* and *about* broaden and change the answer's meaning.

While absolutes and qualifiers are useful clues in multiple-choice answers, they are not absolute guidelines. Sometimes absolutes are, in fact, correct. The statement, "All human life is dependent on water," is absolute. And it's true.

And qualifiers don't always point to a correct answer, either: the qualifier must be correct. For example, the statement, "Most people in the United States are bilingual," contains the qualifier *most*, but it is incorrect. (A better qualified answer would be, "*Many* Americans are bilingual.")

So, absolutes and qualifiers won't automatically tell you if an answer is correct, but you can often use *absolutes* as warning clues that an answer may be wrong and *qualifiers* as similar cues that another choice may be correct.

Here are some commonly used absolutes and qualifiers.

Absolutes—may indicate an incorrect answer:

all, every

no, none

always

never

exactly

perfect

prove

is, are (without any qualification)

will
Qualifiers—may indicate a better answer:

many, most

few

frequently, often, typically

rarely

approximately

suggests, offers evidence that

usually, generally

probably, may, might

Notice above that we said, "Absolutes may indicate an incorrect answer." The word *may* is the qualifier in this sentence.

Use these seven tips and you'll very likely do better on multiple-choice exams.

Four Things to Try When You Don't Have a Clue

Sometimes, despite good preparation, you'll face a question that stumps you. Is there anything you can do with multiple-choice questions that you just don't know?

Yes, several techniques can raise your odds, though they cannot take the place of studying and knowing the subject.

In a typical standardized exam, you'll have five choices. If you just guess at random, chances of being correct are one in five, or only twenty percent. In other words, you're four times more likely to guess wrong than right.

However, if you can change the odds to fifty-fifty, you'll at least have a better chance. Here are tips that may help improve your odds when there's a question that stumps you.

1. *Don't pick an answer you've never heard of.* (This assumes, of course, that you have studied, gone to class regularly, and have at least some familiarity with the subject.)

Creating tests isn't easy. To come up with the necessary number of choices for each multiple-choice question, professors and test writers will often resort to using irrelevant material for some of the incorrect answers. Don't be misled by these irrelevant choices.

2. *If two answers are opposites, one is likely to be right.* This isn't always true, but it will often raise your odds to 50-50.

3. *If one answer includes another, and adds additional information, the more complete answer is often right.* Choose the most complete answer, especially if you know that part of it is correct.

4. *If you know two answers are correct and aren't sure about the third, choose "all of the above."* This is a better guide if the phrase, "all of the above" rarely appears on the test you're taking, and if you can choose only one answer.

Should You Guess?

Students rightly wonder whether to guess on questions that you simply don't know. When you can't eliminate any options and thus raise your odds, should you just guess?

The correct answer is *it depends.*

On many standardized tests, there is a penalty for guessing. That means that a percentage of your wrong answers is subtracted from your correct answers to compute your score.

On teacher-made tests, there is rarely a penalty for guessing, but always ask to be sure. *If there is no penalty, you should guess.*

How do you know which standardized exams penalize wrong answers?

Read the information booklet or online information from the testing company. This information should be easily available online and in your school's testing office.

If there is no penalty for guessing, then you should definitely guess without guilt.

If there is a penalty, follow the guidelines in the test booklet. (*Often, you'll be told to guess only if you can eliminate at least one of the choices.* However, standardized tests vary, so be sure you understand the policy of the exam you're taking.)

Last Steps for Multiple-Choice Exams

When you finish, look back over the exam for obvious omissions. Did you skip any questions by mistake? Did you intend to come back to certain questions if you had the chance? Has an answer suddenly come to you—maybe even from information you picked up from other questions?

Don't change answers unless you have a reason for the change. First impressions are often correct, and random changes will probably do more harm than good.

These tips may help a bit when you're really unsure of an answer, but they are not intended to replace solid studying and good preparation. *You'll do well on tests if you know the material.* It's really that simple. To repeat: the best test-taking technique is to study the material well.

Twelve Ways to Excel on Essay Exams

Many teachers and professors are convinced that essay or discussion questions do a better job of measuring what you know than multiple-choice tests. After all, on an essay, you have to come up with *all* the information yourself and organize and present it.

That can make these exams more difficult.

Thus, when you write an essay, your task is much more complex than in multiple-choice exams. To write a good answer to an discussion question, here's what you have to do:

First, you need to *remember the facts and information* you need. Only rarely will you be able to use notes or have an open-book exam. Usually you'll be depending on what you know.

Next, you'll have to *organize these facts* clearly. This, for many students, is difficult. However, if you know the subject well, it will be easier to organize your answer logically and you'll be able to write a much better answer.

Writing the exam will draw on your command of the language and your writing skills. You usually won't have time to do more than one version of an answer, so it will help if you develop a *good sense of org*anization.

Your professor will look for a premise, supporting facts, and a conclusion, and these require the ability to put your thoughts in order.

Frankly, that's a lot, and you'll rarely have the luxury of extra time, so the following ideas will be helpful.

Prepare For Essay Exams as You Study

First, use these two tips *as you study*:

1. *Try to predict* the kinds of questions that will be on the exam. You're studying by self-testing already. Now, as you study specifically for an essay exam, try to devise questions like those you'll see on the test.

What was emphasized in the professor's lectures? Were there clues such as, "This is very important," or, "Pay special attention to this handout?" Don't forget the big picture that's conveyed by the name of the class and the emphasis from the syllabus.

So, as you study actively by self-testing as described in chapter 12, turn statements into questions. You'll be learning better and preparing for exams at the same time.

2. *Rehearse, rehearse, rehearse* the answers. When you've created realistic sample questions, be sure you can answer them completely. That means you'll have to know the supporting material, facts, and arguments for the answer.

You can practice your answers orally, which is much faster than writing them out. Think through your answers to be sure they're focused and organized, and rehearse them till you're satisfied that you've mastered the material.

While you may not want to write out practice answers for routine exams, you may find it very helpful to make outline-type lists of your facts and be sure that your organization is appropriate.

Twelve Tips to Use During The Exam

Now that you're prepared, have studied actively, have predicted questions, and rehearsed your answers, here are twelve tips that can help you during essay exams.

1. *Read the directions* for each question. Sometimes there is a choice, so don't leap to conclusions. Perhaps the question says, "Answer *one* of the following." If you are skimming the question quickly, you may unnecessarily answer all parts of the question, and waste valuable time.

Also note how many points each question is worth, and allocate your time based on that information. Thus, spend about half your time on a 50-point question, and less on one that's worth only 10 points.

2. *Underline key terms* as you read each question. Of course you can't do this on a computer-based exam, so it may be necessary to jot down the main terms on scratch paper.

Why is this helpful? It works because it *forces* you to focus on exactly what is being asked. If a question has several parts, put numbers by each one so you won't forget any of them.

It's possible to write a great essay that doesn't match the question. So be sure to read each question completely and *be sure you respond to what is being asked.*

3. *Plan your essay.* Don't just start writing wildly. Take a minute to gather your thoughts. List the points you want to include. Then number them to make a quick outline of your answer. Sometimes a minute or two spent brainstorming will help you remember the facts you need.

Don't just lump everything together. You're being graded on your ability to *organize* what you know and put it in the proper perspective. If you have time, it will be useful to make a very quick outline, listing your main topics and your primary supporting points.

So, start with a main point, and then provide supporting data.

4. *Pay attention to the VERBS* in each question. They tell you what you're supposed to do. *List and explain* is very different from *compare and contrast.*

5. *Many successful students commonly rephrase the wording of the question to begin an answer.* This is a very useful tip and not an ironclad rule, of course, but it really helps focus your thoughts on what the question is actually asking.

Thus, if the question is, "Describe the ecosystem of a small pond," your answer might begin like this, "In the ecosystem of a small pond there are several subsystems that are complex and codependent."

This approach offers two real advantages for starting essay answers. First, it keeps you from getting stuck as you think about how to begin. It's an almost automatic way to get started.

And, more importantly, it forces you to *answer the question that is being asked*, and helps keep you from going off on an unrelated tangent.

6. *Make the important points in your answer stand out.* Underline key concepts and start a new paragraph when you introduce a new point. Make it easy for your professor to see that you know the material.

In this book, we use subheads, italics, bold text, quotation marks, and numbered lists to make important points stand out. As you write, do the same with your answer. Underline for emphasis or make a numbered list.

Whatever you do, *don't write a long answer as one unending paragraph.*

Even if your answer has some good points, if they are buried in one long paragraph, your professor may find it hard to spot them. Your job in answering an essay question is very much like any writer's job: you want to keep the reader interested.

And, in this case, the reader is also giving you a grade. So, make it interesting and easy to read.

7. Use transitional and connective words to help your answer flow properly and to avoid the deadly "one long paragraph" approach used by so many students.

Words like *first, thus, later, therefore* and similar transitional expressions help guide the reader through your thinking, and your paper. They may also show that you understand sequence, history, or cause-and-effect.

You'll find that using such connective words can quickly improve your writing, and it shows the professor that your thinking is coherent and orderly.

8. *Write your essay so it's easy to read.* Don't irritate instructors or graders with sloppy, illegible handwriting, messy scratched-out places, or a microscopic scrawl. By the time your professor grades all the essays from all his or her classes, a well-written, neat paper will really be appreciated.

In fact, college experiments have consistently shown that neatly-written exams are graded higher than sloppy, hard-to-read ones. Assuming you type well, this is one advantage of computer-based exams: at least the grader can read them!

Here are some strategies that will help make your essay exams more readable:

a. Write as neatly as you can.

b. Use erasable ink.

c. Use numbers and underlining for emphasis. In this book, we frequently use lists (like this one) to make the points stand out, and you should, too.

d. Write on only one side of the page, unless you are writing in a blue-book and are instructed to use both sides.

e. Leave space in the margin for comments.

f. Use copy paper or your three-ring binder paper, rather than spiral-bound paper, which is messy.

9. *Don't use abbreviations in essay answers*. In an age when much of your writing automatically includes abbreviations for texting, this may be difficult to remember, but it's important.

Abbreviations are great for taking notes and sending text messages, *but not for writing essays.*

10. *Proofread your answers if you have time*. If you finish an exam early, don't be the first to rush out of the room, but take the time to read over your answers for omissions, spelling and usage errors, and obvious goofs. Erase stray messy marks. Be sure your name is on each page.

You'll be amazed at how much you can improve your answer by simply reading over it before turning it in. (In fact, this is true for virtually everything you write, including emails. A quick re-read will often show that you didn't really say what you thought you said!)

11. If you're running out of time, quickly *list the points you would have included*. This will at least show the instructor that you knew more than you were able to write.

I remember an essay in a graduate course for which I actually got full credit for an answer, even though I ran out of time and couldn't finish the exam. I hurriedly made an outline of what I would have included, and it satisfied the professor.

12. *Never leave a question blank.* Always write *something* for each answer. Even if your answer is really poor, you'll likely get some credit.

But an omitted answer gets none.

What to Do If You Don't Have a Clue

Sometimes, however, despite your best preparation, you'll be faced with an unexpected question that you just don't know. What should you do?

If you're drawing a complete blank, first, stop for a moment to calm yourself down.

Then, try brainstorming and free-associating on the topic.

Use scratch paper and list *everything* you can think of that *might* relate to the question. Often, you'll be surprised at what you can come up with. Then write as good an answer as you can from those notes.

Remember: *a blank answer gets no credit.*

Even if you're drawing an absolute blank, a poor answer will usually be much better than no answer at all. Blank spaces leave big, glaring holes that leap out at the grader.

PLS Action Step 16

This is a pop test. Take a blank sheet of paper, and write a short essay on the following question. Don't look at your notes or this book.

Describe the proper procedure for writing a good essay for an exam. Be specific and include as many of the twelve points discussed in this section as possible.

Grade your answer by comparing it to the process described in this chapter. Include the format, neatness, clarity, organization and content of your answer as you assess how you did.

If your essay doesn't satisfy you, review this chapter.

This PLS Step is not a theoretical exercise. You WILL have essay exams over new material. Use these techniques, and you'll write better answers and get better grades.

Chapter 15

How to Manage Test Anxiety

Do you have problems with test anxiety? Do you feel so apprehensive when you take an exam that your performance—and your grade—is affected?

If so, use the strategies in this chapter to help manage this problem.

(And if you really struggle with tests, you may want to visit your school's counseling center for personal help. Most colleges have professionals available to work with students who experience severe anxiety, and such serious problems are beyond the scope of this book.)

First, recognize that *some anxiety is good*.

A little stress helps focus your attention, and probably motivates you to study more diligently than you might otherwise. Our stress-reduction goal is not to turn you into a happy-go-lucky student who doesn't care about exams.

After all, tests *are* important, so you'll always feel some pressure.

However, if anxiety, nervousness, and stress interfere with your ability to show what you know, here are three strategies that have helped many students I've worked with.

What Triggers Your Test Anxiety?

First, *identify situations that trigger your anxiety*. These will not be the same for all students.

Often, specific situations may cause you to feel nervous during an exam. If you can identify these specific *triggers*, you can take steps to change them.

Here are three examples of things that might trigger test anxiety for you. Note that the suggested solutions aren't complicated, but they are quite effective.

Trigger 1: Hearing other students talk about the exam or their studying routines makes you feel nervous and unprepared.

Solution: Find a way to avoid those people before a test. Arrange to arrive right on time, talk with other friends, or change the subject when someone mentions an exam.

If you've prepared, chances are that you know as much (or maybe more) than other students, so you'll gain nothing by listening to their conversation about what they expect from the test or how much they've studied.

By chance, one of the excellent students we interviewed in Chapter 17, Katherine, mentioned how she would "freak out" when she listened to her friends talk before exams, so she changed her schedule on test days to avoid such conversations.

Trigger 2: When other students finish an exam before you do, you worry that they know more and have done better on the test. This raises your anxiety as you finish the exam.

Solution: Remind yourself that different people work at different speeds. Maybe the early finishers just write faster than you do. (Or perhaps they finish early because they didn't study and had nothing to say!)

Trigger 3: Sounds distract you. Once you notice them you may have a hard time getting your mind back on the exam. On computer-based tests, the clatter of many keyboards can be bothersome to some people, for example.

Solution: Sometimes, you can move to a different place in the room —a simple solution if the problem is, for example, sounds from the hallway or an outside window, or another student who chews gum audibly or wears jangly jewelry.

Or, you can buy a set of inexpensive earplugs, though you should practice wearing them before the test to get used to the way they feel in your ears. These earplugs are available in many pharmacies and at sporting-good stores (in the hunting section).

(A large selection of earplugs is available online and may be worth checking out if you're bothered by noise. Search for "musicians' earplugs," which don't block out ALL the sound but just reduce the volume. And they're easier to use than the inexpensive foam design.)

Exams are, by their nature, stressful events and if you can easily control these, and other, outside *triggers*, you'll remove needless sources of extra anxiety.

Use Physical Approaches to Combat Anxiety

Sometimes watching what you eat and drink before exams can make a big difference. And, surprisingly, adding some physical exercise before a test can also be very helpful.

Problem: You feel edgy, nervous, irritable, and sometimes even weak during exams, so it is difficult for you to concentrate.

Solution a: Be careful what you eat and drink before tests. Sugar and caffeine make many people edgy and irritable. Remember that soft drinks contain a lot of caffeine *and* sugar, so try to avoid them, as well as too much coffee, chocolate, and tea.

There is, for many students, a natural tendency to drink more coffee than usual to be "extra alert" for an exam, but too much caffeine (and sugar) can quickly become counterproductive. Know your limits, and know how you react to these stimulants.

(This is particularly true for "sports drinks" and "energy drinks." While the caffeine boost may be helpful in some situations, it's easy to overdo it and become agitated and jittery.)

Balance is the answer with caffeine.

It's also helpful to eat balanced meals before exams, with plenty of protein and carbohydrates, to be sure of a good supply of energy without the ups and downs typically caused by the caffeine/sugar rush.

If you are taking a very long exam, such as the GRE, you may need to take an energy bar or some other low-sugar snack to help control your blood-sugar levels. While you won't be able to eat during the exam, you probably can during break times.

Don't overlook this aspect of long exams if your metabolism is accustomed to regular meals and snacks. If you don't normally go for four hours, for example, without eating, doing so during an exam may be difficult or distracting to you—but once you're aware of it, this is an easy problem to fix.

Solution b: Exercise before an exam. Often, walking for twenty to thirty minutes will calm you down and give you a relaxed feeling as you enter the test room.

Many students who have taken my seminars and workshops report that a walk around the campus or in a nearby park helps clear their minds and gives them a sense of being in control before an exam.

And, it's usually better than frantic last-minute cramming, which often increases both your anxiety and confusion levels.

You've probably heard the expression, "runner's high," that describes the euphoria athletes experience after exercise. Scientific research demonstrates that vigorous exercise releases chemicals called *endorphins* in the brain. It further shows that the amount of endorphins produced correlates with athletes' feelings of euphoria.

Since you can't feel euphoric and anxious at the same time, these brain chemicals serve as natural relaxants, and exercise is a great way to produce them.

A Physical Approach That Worked

A graduate student in one of my study-skills workshops told us about the experience she'd had with exercise before exams.

She was taking a demanding psychology class and had experienced severe test anxiety during the first exam. But, by chance, her weekly racquetball game was scheduled shortly before the mid-term, so she played a hard game of racquetball, showered, and went straight to the test.

This time, unlike her experience during the first exam, she had absolutely *no* test anxiety. The endorphins that had been released during her racquetball game kept her totally relaxed during the two-hour test.

It was such a remarkable change that she told my workshop about it. In fact, she told us that she is now scheduling a racquetball game before every big exam!

Change How You Think About Exams

Use *positive self-talk* to help control test anxiety.

Problem: Negative thoughts or self-talk do you in. Many students put more and more pressure on themselves by thinking stress-building thoughts. "This exam is really crucial to my future and I absolutely MUST do well on it," is the kind of thinking that can be counter-productive.

Solution: Of course, it may be true that a particular exam is very important, but how you present the test to yourself, or how you "frame" it, can really have an enormous impact on your stress level.

Don't view tests as traps. Try to see them as a chance to show off what you know, to demonstrate to the professor what you've learned and how clearly you can express it. (And, if you're using the reading and study tips from this book, your answers should reflect a high level of learning about the subject.)

So, rather than tell yourself how tough the test is, how worried you are, and how crucial a good grade is, try positive self talk. Say things like this, "Okay, I feel really good about this exam because I've prepared well. I'm ready to show what I know."

When you think this way, you may actually find that you enjoy exams. Why not? When you're prepared, you know you'll do well.

And here's the bottom line: you can't make an 'A' unless you take the exam. Like many college students I've worked with, you'll find that when you *take control of how you approach tests*, you'll be able to reduce (or even eliminate) test anxiety.

PLS Action Step 17

Start a list of things that *trigger* test anxiety for you. Leave plenty of space between the items on this list.

Then, devise *your own strategy* for coping with each problem.

Pay special attention to the physical and self-talk aspects of test-stress. How can you change what you eat and what you say to yourself to improve your reaction to stress?

Can you build in some exercise before an exam? What kind? Where? Be specific as you think about how you might use thie approach. emember: simple strategies usually work best.

When you identify workable, practical solutions, write them down in your *PLS* notebook. And next time you have an exam, use these strategies. You'll be surprised how effective they can be.

PART FOUR: BONUS TIPS FOR COLLEGE SUCCESS

Twenty-One More Things You Should Know

Tips from Seven Successful College Students

Making A's—Onward and Upward

Eleven Commandments for College Success

Chapter 16

Twenty-One More Useful Things You Should Know

Now you know a lot about how to improve concentration, get organized, manage your time, take great notes in class, read effectively, study smart, take tests wisely, and manage test anxiety.

All the techniques and strategies in the book come from my experience helping thousands of college students learn to be successful students. The ideas I've presented all work, and can give you both the *support* skills and the *academic* skills that every student needs.

But there's more.

So, here are 21 bonus tips that didn't fit into the main subject categories of this book. Some may seem minor, and some may seem obvious, but they are important, they work, and these ideas will help you succeed in a competitive college environment.

These are twenty-one *practical* tips that you can begin using today.

Tip #1 *Go to class.*

Many convincing studies have shown that the *best predictor of college grades is simply class attendance.*

It's not difficult to see why this is true: if you miss class, you'll need to somehow find out what you've missed and catch up on that day's work before you can move on.

So, simply missing class makes it easy to fall behind, and *once you're behind, it takes extra effort to catch up.*

This is so simple that you may be surprised to see it here, and you may think that it's perfectly evident for several reasons.

Aside from the obvious danger of falling behind in class, you're wasting money, too—maybe lots of money.

To make this clear, it helps to do a little math and figure out what each class session is costing you or your family.

Recently, we calculated that tuition (only) for each class meeting at an elite Ivy League school costs $178, based on 2 class meetings a week. At a large mid-west state university, the per-class cost works out to $107.That's a LOT of money to waste each time you cut a class.

You know how many classes you're taking and what you're paying for tuition. It's not difficult to compute the per-class-meeting cost, and it's a worthwhile exercise to do.

(And this is an even more sobering thought if you're borrowing money for college. Interest on student loans can add a LOT to your total cost. *Why throw money down the drain and increase your loan totals for something you didn't even use?*)

But it's absolutely true that distractions abound, and on cold, rainy mornings it can be really hard to get up and out for an early class. Good students make the extra effort--and their grades show it.

Tip #2 Get *personal help if you need it.*

There are many differences between high-school and college, but perhaps the main one is the amount of responsibility that college students are expected to assume.

No one will make you do your work, and no one will stand over you to be sure you do your best—as your parents or teachers probably did in high school.

So now you'll have to find the necessary resources and drive *within yourself.*

Sometimes you may have real problems outside the classroom that affect your performance (and your life), so be sure to let your professors and your adviser know if this is the case.

Sickness, depression, family crises, financial difficulty, or a divorce are all stressful, and your professors should know if you are dealing with these or other troublesome situations.

Most colleges and universities have counseling centers that offer help for the stresses of college life, so if you're having a problem, talk to your professors and locate help on campus. It's there for you.

In college you may be on your own for the first time, but *there is no need to face extreme difficulties alone.* If you need it, look for help, and you'll find it and benefit from it.

Tip #3 *Sit at the front of each class if you have a choice.*

This is an easy one, and seems almost too simple to mention, but it really matters WHERE you choose to sit in a class.

University studies consistently show that *where you sit* in class can have a lot to do with your grades. Plus, if you sit up front, you'll hear better, see the board or monitor better, not be distracted by other students, and be less tempted to use your electronic gadgets in full view of the professor.

Tip #4 *Get to know your professors and always show them common courtesy.*

Professors and instructors are human and they react positively or negatively (just as anyone would) to rude class behavior from students. We are not advising insincerity at all—that is usually obvious and may be counterproductive anyway.

What we ARE saying is that common courtesy and politeness will go a long way in college. And in life.

Yes, professors are paid to teach, and yes, some are much better and more interesting teachers than others. But all will expect you to pay attention in class, not be distracting to others, do your assignments, and learn the material.

After all, that's why you are in college in the first place.

It should be obvious, but don't talk with fellow students during lectures. Don't make it obvious if you're bored, and for goodness' sake, don't go to sleep. And it's not good practice to take meals into class—it's distracting to you, your classmates, and the instructor.

Similarly, don't talk on your cellphone, don't surf the web, and don't text during a lecture. You (or your parents) are paying a lot of money so you can be in this classroom, so *be there* during class hours.

We described earlier how a prospective student at one of the country's finest MBA programs was flagged as "do not admit" simply because he spent an entire class visit fooling with his iPhone.

An informal poll of several professors and instructors and asked what student activities are most bothersome to them. Electronic distraction was at the top of the list. If you simply must make a call or text someone, have the courtesy to leave the classroom to make your contact.

On the positive side, *participate* when you are in class.

Ask questions, and don't worry about seeming dumb. If you don't understand something, you can be sure that other students are confused, too.

Professors will always appreciate and encourage your involvement. And if you're engaged, you'll learn more.

Tip #5 *Get enough sleep.*

There is a lot do to in college. There are wonderful new opportunities, new friends, new social life, and lots of new freedom for most students. It's useful to remember, though, that *regular sleep actually enhances thinking and learning*.

Make an effort to get the sleep you need every night. Remember that different people need different amounts of sleep to function at their best, and you may need more than your roommate.

You'll find it easier to learn and retain what you've studied if you get the amount of sleep that's right for you. As John Medina says in *Brain Rules*, "Sleep loss cripples thinking . . . Loss of sleep hurts attention, executive function, working memory, mood, quantitative skills, logical reasoning, and even motor dexterity."

What's more, studies, such as show that while you are asleep, your brain is processing what you learned earlier in the day and making it easier for you to remember what you've studied.

Getting the right amount of sleep is one more way to study smarter and not harder.

Tip #6 *Be neat and write legibly.*

Read over papers that you turn in for obvious usage or grammar errors, and be sure spell-check is turned on (but don't rely on it completely. Spell check won't know whether you intended to use *to, two*, or *too*.)

If you turn in handwritten class work or exams, be sure your work can be read easily.

In math and science classes, especially, you can know the material, follow the correct procedures and formulas, and still get no credit for your answer because you misread a **7** for a **2**, or a **3** for an **8**.

Such careless errors can cost you a good grade, and for a*bsolutely no reason.*

Tip #7 D*o extra reading.*

This is an enjoyable way to get ahead in college. Visit the library, bookstore, or download supplementary reading to your Kindle or other ebook reader. You'll find non-fiction books, novels, newspapers, magazines, journals, and blogs to be filled with more information on whatever you're studying.

For example, you can find historical novels for virtually any era of history—the Civil War, the Crusades, Colonial America or first-century Rome.

Such reading will add interesting facts, background, and insight especially to literature and history classes. It can be a good way to get the bigger picture in your mind and to understand the context for what you're studying.

And, online resources, in particular, can keep you up-to-the minute on new developments in any field. As you move from general studies to a major field of interest, be sure you follow the blogs, websites, twitter feeds, and publications that are most important to your special area of study.

College is unlike high school in this important way: your professors may assume that you're interested and knowledgeable. It's often up to you to bring yourself up to the expected level of achievement . . . or to surpass it. Extra reading is the route to this success.

A good way to think about your college experience is to *see how much you can learn, not how little you can get by with.*

Tip #8 *Build a powerful vocabulary.*

A good vocabulary makes you a more educated person, and will help you do better on the GRE, LSAT, MCAT and all the other standardized tests you may need to take. Large sections of all these exams are based on your understanding of words, and this is an area where educated people never stop learning.

What's more, a limited vocabulary can be embarrassing. What would you do if a professor asks you a question and you don't know what her words mean? Or if someone uses a word you don't know in a class discussion?

You could, of course, get through life with a minimal vocabulary, and millions of people do, but you'd miss so much. The more words you know, the sharper your thinking will be and the better you'll appreciate the world around you.

How do you build a powerful vocabulary? Of course, you can buy excellent vocabulary-building books and use word-a-day apps.

You can (and should) subscribe to daily email services or blogs that present and discuss a new word every day. That's easy and fun. Just search for "word a day email." And, of course, there are apps that do the same thing.

Here's a simple and effective way to build your vocabulary is to *actively notice all the new words you see in your reading*, including textbooks, novels, magazines, newspapers and websites.

When you encounter a new word in your actual reading, it's likely to be the kind of word you need to know, so write it on an index card and define it on the back.

Review these cards frequently, and *make it a point to use each new word in conversation several times* within a week. Then, you'll really *know* it and that new word will be yours.

(Since you now know how memory works, and the crucial value of repetition and rehearsal, you now understand why it's important to *use the new words* you're learning. It's practicing what we've learned in this book.)

You can also list new words on the back blank page of a book (if it's yours) or on a paper bookmark.

And one advantage of reading ebooks is that their built-in dictionaries make it easy to instantly check any word you don't know. Just place the cursor (or your finger) on a word, and the dictionary will be easily accessible.

By training yourself to notice the *kinds of words that authors actually use,* you'll be organically building your vocabulary every day (and preparing yourself for the vocabulary-intensive graduate-school exams in your future, too).

Tip #9 *Be an extra-credit student.*

Go the extra mile and see how much you can do and how much you can learn. If you're in school full-time, *this may be the last chance in your life to make learning a full-time job.*

If your professors give you the option of doing an extra-credit project or answering an extra test question, do it. Even if your grades are good, extra-credit is like insurance.

Some professors actually reserve A's for students who do extra assignments and go beyond the average, and many instructors also offer extra-credit options to help raise your grades.

Tip #10 *Don't fall behind—do something for each class each day.*

Perhaps this should have been tip number one, because it's so important. Take steps to be sure that you don't fall behind in difficult classes, because it's like falling into a hole that gets deeper and deeper every day.

In fact, many students fall behind because they simply miss classes. This could be because you're out with the flu, or because you just didn't go to class on a beautiful spring day, or because you partied too much the night before.

In any case, you'll need to find out what you missed and add that to your study load. Be sure to check with a fellow student to see what happened in class, so you can return without an overwhelming amount of catch-up work to do.

Be especially careful not to fall behind in foreign language, programming, science, or math classes where today's lecture often builds on a clear grasp of yesterday's work. It's very easy to quickly become hopelessly lost in these fast-moving classes.

From our earlier discussion of how memory works, you know that keeping up is the best way to learn, giving your brain plenty of review and "down time" to move new information into permanent memory.

When you are particularly busy, you'll often be tempted to ignore one class to prepare for an exam in another. This can be a dangerous and self-defeating path, and can quickly lead to a teeter-totter-like attempt to keep your studies balanced. Here's why:

If you ignore class A to prepare for class B, the work from A doesn't go away; it just builds up and you fall behind.

Then, when you're caught up in class B, you're behind in A. And now you're tempted to ignore B while you catch up in A. And maybe classes C and D have suffered during the balancing act, too.

This is a downward spiral that just doesn't work. So do what you can to stay current and not fall behind. It's much better to try very hard to keep up-to-date with each class.

Do something for each class every day.

For a fascinating real-world example of how this works, do a Google search for "Jerry Seinfeld and procrastination." The highly successful comedian has a simple explanation for how to succeed and beat procrastination, and it (essentially) is this: work on your projects EVERY day. *Don't break the daily chain*!

Of course, you're not a world-famous comedian—you're a college student, but the principle will work for you as well as it does for him. This is a Google search you really should do because you'll be inspired by Seinfeld's simple but powerful productivity tips.

Tip #11 *Use outside resources* that can help you master challenging material.

If you are taking an extremely difficult class, you may find it very beneficial to seek extra help. Perhaps the professor offers extra *discussion groups*, or you might locate more advanced students who can tutor you.

And, if you are having real problems in a particular class, don't keep it a secret from your professor. You won't be the only student who is struggling, nor the first, and there will usually be an array of resources to help you.

Sometimes *online resources*, such as iTunes U and Khan Academy, and even YouTube can be of great benefit.

In fact, the Khan Academy, as one example, is such an astounding free resource that you should at least visit the site (www.khanacademy.org) to become familiar with the wide range of free, very helpful, specifically-targeted videos available there.

Khan Academy is a growing collection of hundreds of short, clear, understandable videos on many subjects (with emphasis on math, economics, and science), and it has helped many, many thousands of students understand complex problems.

Tutors can be very helpful, too, especially with subjects like languages, science, and math that build sequentially on earlier knowledge. Often, colleges will offer tutoring through the counselor's office or the learning assistance center.

Or, you can locate a private tutor to give you a personal boost. Graduate students can be a good source. Ask your counselor or instructor for suggestions, and often each department maintains lists of qualified tutors.

A few hours spent with a good tutor can unlock the mysteries of math concepts, or improve your Mandarin pronunciation, or help you grasp complex accounting principles.

You don't have to re-invent the wheel. Many students have been along the same path you are traveling, and there are plenty of resources to help, if you'll look for them.

Tip #12 *Take advantage of summers and long vacations.*

You can often use this time away from school to gain background and knowledge for classes you'll be taking later. Here are three ideas that will help you return to class ahead of the game:

1. *Read widely* in your field during your vacation months. Even in our digitally-distracted age, reading is the way to build deep knowledge, and the success of your college career will depend to a large degree on reading.

If you've declared your major, you'll know what to read, but you might even stop by next-semester's professor to ask for suggestions.

And reading for fun can be helpful, too. If you're reading medical adventure fiction, for example, you'll be gaining background that may be helpful in biology or anatomy classes. And historical novels can enjoyably add a human dimension to history classes.

2. *Pursue a special interest* through jobs or internships. This will help you use vacation time to become more expert in your field, or to explore an area to see how it fits your interest.

For example, we know a student who was planning to apply to vet school until she spent a summer working in an animal hospital and found that it didn't really suit her aptitudes and interests. She's now in law school, but might have made a big career mistake without spending that summer in the local veterinary hospital.

Of course, you can find a paying job for the summer, and that is often necessary. If possible, try to work in the area you're planning to enter after college because you'll learn a lot—and a good summer job or internship can bring you very useful contacts.

3. Use your vacation time to prepare actively for the GRE or other exams you know you'll be taking.

Get a book of practice tests, sign up for online test preparation, or take a test-preparation class. You'll add to your knowledge, and you'll become familiar with the style and format of the tests. You'll see where you need more work and more review.

It *would not be smart to take these difficult exams without lots of preparation*, so some summer study of test-prep books can pay off in a BIG way later on.

Rather than depend on last-minute (and expensive) cram courses for these tests, spread your preparation over several months.

And, to repeat a theme of this book, this *steady* approach to learning uses what we know about how memory actually works.

Tip #13 *Get really familiar with your college library.*

Most college and university libraries offer introductory classes and orientation sessions. You'll probably get a quick tour during orientation week, but if the library also offers more in-depth classes or workshops, be sure to take them.

The library is a major resource at every college that's easy to overlook, and the better you know it, the more you'll get from it. Good students learn to use the college library inside-out.

Librarians today are highly trained information specialists, and they know how to find things through incredible printed and online sources that you might never know about without their assistance.

They know their way around books, magazines, journals, printed reference material, annuals, reports, government documents, vertical files, on-line databases of all sorts, special subscription websites, and much more.

Get to know them and let them help as you go through your college years.

You'll probably have access to student-only online resources, too, and that's part of what your tuition buys. Use these resources; they are there for you.

And, when you are looking for a good, quiet place to study, you may find a study carrel or table in the library that is away from distractions. (But, as mentioned before, the larger tables on the main floor often become social centers, and several of the successful students' tips in the next chapter repeat this point.)

Tip #14 *Learn to type well.*

Of course you've been using computers, phones and tablets since you were a child and you doubtlessly know your way around a keyboard. But most likely, you just learned to type by doing it, and there may be much room for improvement.

Since so much of what you do, including online essay exams, is dependent on your keyboard skills, take the time to be sure you're (literally) up to speed.

There are dozens of computer-based typing improvement programs , apps, and games, and if you can raise both speed and accuracy, you'll be doing yourself a *big* favor.

True, many applications are moving toward voice input, but fluen t and accurate typing is a skill that you'll need for the rest of your life, take the time to improve it now if you think you need it.

Tip #15 *Develop as many computer skills as you can.*

You never know what you'll need in future semesters or later when you leave college. And college can be a terrific place to improve your computer skills because you often have access to labs with all the latest programs—and expert staff there to help you, too.

For instance, we know of a local university with a large computer lab called "The Digital Aquarium" where computers loaded with the very latest photographic, layout, design and animation programs are available to all students.

These programs would likely be prohibitively expensive for most students, but in college you can take the time (and maybe a class) to learn Excel, Photoshop, InDesign, Sibelius, Finale or other specialized software without having to pay lots of money for the program or subscription.

This kind of accessibility to programs, labs, and expert teachers is a resource that will rarely be easily available to you when you leave school. Take advantage of it while you can because you just don't know what you'll need to know later.

Here's an example: a student in one of my classes complained about having to learn a complex relational database program. He's a musician and saw no need for taking time to master this many-layered, difficult-to-learn software. But when he applied for an internship at a major recording studio, he was stunned to find that the studio used that very database program daily as its base of operations and expected all employees to know it.

He didn't get the internship.

True, programs come and go, what's hot today maybe be old news tomorrow, and programming languages change too. Today's top graphic design program may be supplanted in a few years with a new one, but you'll do yourself big favors if you become familiar with as many programs as you can.

Don't forget, too, that while you're a student you can often buy software at major educational discounts. You may want to buy or subscribe to Photoshop, Office, or other programs before you graduate so you can get the deeply discounted student rate.

(Check the fine print before buying, however. You may find that discounted educational editions cannot be updated as new versions of the software are developed. Or these less-expensive versions may come with other limiting restrictions.)

Finally, stay at least broadly up-to-date with what's happening in technology. No, every student doesn't need to be a geek, and you don't have to learn to code (thought it certainly won't hurt), but you should be aware of trends and major new developments because they will have daily impact on your life.

Tip #16 *Eat right and get enough exercise.*

You've heard this until it's a cliché, but it's true. Your mind can't function at its best if you're not in good shape.

Study after study shows a *direct* relationship between nutrition and mental ability, so eat a balanced diet for optimum health.

Sometimes a muti-vitamin is good insurance if you find yourself eating a lot of fast food, or you're under excess stress. The field of nutrition is changing rapidly, so keep up with new developments that could affect, and potentially improve, your life.

In college, you may have an "all-you-can-eat" meal plan, or be surrounded by poor choices in a food court, and there's no one looking over your shoulder to be sure you take care of yourself.

It's now up to you, so remember: *you are what you eat.*

Health professionals are concerned that many students in the United States are destined for major health problems later in life because of obesity and lack of exercise.

Diabetes is just one of the debilitating diseases that can often be avoided by developing good eating and exercise habits.

The good news here is that most colleges offer an array of pleasant options for getting that needed exercise, from swimming pools and workout rooms to hikes and canoe trips, so investigate what your school offers. You may be pleasantly surprised at the wide range of activities and facilities that are available to use and enjoy while you improve your health.

And, when you join these groups, you'll make new friends as you exercise, too.

Tip #17 *Do what you can to stay well.*

If you're sick and miss lots of classes, you'll find it difficult or impossible to catch up.

Research seems to show that plenty of sleep is vital, as is adequate vitamin D, exercise, and (again) a balanced diet.

But you can't live in a bubble, and in classes and groups you'll be exposed to plenty of bacteria and viruses, so take steps to protect yourself. Try not to sit next to a student who is clearly sick.

Remember that *surfaces* such as desks, library tables, door handles, shared computer keyboards and so on may be collectors of germs, so it's helpful to get in the habit of *frequent hand-washing*—with hot water.

It's easy to find current articles that exploresthe importance of hand-washing to prevent colds. This is another simple habit that can really pay off.

Also, doctors say that colds are often spread by touching the eyes and nose, so try to minimize that tendency if you have it.

Lots of students carry a small bottle of hand-sanitizing gel in their backpacks, and this is a good idea, especially during flu season. It's one way doctors and nurses who work in hospitals keep from getting sick all the time, and if it works for them, it can work for you, too.

If you do get sick, don't go to class and expose the rest of the group. It's better to ask someone to take notes for you or to record the lecture.

Your college will have some kind of on-site health services that are available if you need a doctor or nurse. Large institutions have fully-staffed infirmaries, while smaller schools may have only a staff nurse.

If you think you are really getting sick, don't hesitate to take advantage of the help your college provides.

Tip #18 *Don't cheat yourself by being digitally distracted.*

I've talked about this several times before, but it's so vital that I'm repeating it here.

Today's students face unprecedented and addictive distractions from all kinds of electronic and digital devices. They're fun, they're exciting, they're involving, they connect you instantly to your friends and the world—*but they also keep your mind from focusing and concentrating on the task you're doing.*

Remember the student quoted earlier from a *New York Times* story on digitally-distracted students who said, "When I'm spending hours on Facebook, I have the feeling that I'm busy, doing something really important."

Hours spent on social networks connecting with your friends may *feel* busy and productive (and it's undoubtedly fun to stay in touch), but it is stealing time from your real job in college—which is learning and preparing yourself for a good future.

One student told me, "I use the timer on my phone when I'm having trouble focusing on difficult textbook material because I know that I'll be constantly tempted. I set it for 15 or 20 minutes, and absolutely don't look at my phone until the alarm rings. Then I re-set the timer and have another uninterrupted period of study."

This may not be the ideal way to learn, but it's a lot better than compulsively checking your phone or laptop every few minutes. *You have to give your brain time to learn if you hope to do well in college.*

The same thing goes for TV. If you want to watch a program, by all means watch it, but *don't try to study at the same time*. Your brain isn't designed to function that way. So, don't let TV (or Twitter, Instagram, Snap, or video games) steal college success from you.

We absolutely are not saying to cut yourself off from your online community. You can be a great student and be completely connected, but the success secret is to *keep the digital distractions away from your study time.*

If you do this, you'll do better in class—and you won't feel guilty about your digital relaxation.

Tip #19 *Safeguard your computer and other electronics.*

Don't forget about anti-virus and anti-spam software, surge protectors, and so on. Your dorm may have excellent surge protectors in place, but you should find out for sure. Even the best surge protector may not provide enough security in a violent thunderstorm, so be alert.

Be alert, too, when you're out with your laptop, netbook, iPad or smartphone. If you lose your computer, you'll spend hours and hours trying to reconstruct it and salvage your work. A little time spent thinking about your computer's physical security can be a big time-saver in the long run.

Needless to say, a laptop, cellphone, iPad or other device is extremely attractive to thieves. It can be aggravating to pack up your computer when you leave your library table to go to the restroom, but unless a friend will be there to watch it, you probably should.

This varies by campus, of course, and I've watched students casually (and confidently) leave backpacks and laptop bags piled on the floor outside the cafeteria at a small college in rural Minnesota —something that just wouldn't happen at a large university.

So, know your surroundings, but also be alert. The smaller your device, the quicker it can disappear.

Be aware that airports are often very active sites for thieves who specialize in laptops and other electronics. Watch your things like a hawk as you go through security and yell at the top of your voice if someone picks up your laptop as it comes through the scanner while you are stuck back in the line.

So, when you travel be alert and aware and you might avoid hours (or weeks) of frustration just by keeping your laptop safe.

Experienced travelers also know to be extra careful at airport food courts and in restrooms.

Before you got to college, a friend or family member may have been your tech guru and taken care of your computer. Now it's up to you.

Tip #20 *Don't plagiarize.*

If you're reading this book, you're probably not a student who would buy a term-paper online, but it's good to remember that plagiarism comes in many forms.

A simple copy and paste of information from a web resource is very easy to do, but if you don't attribute the source, it's plagiarism.

Your school will have a strict policy on copying, *and you should be familiar with it because it may cover more much than you'd think.*

Your professors will have no patience with plagiarism, since it is the opposite of why you are in college in the first place. And instructors are surprisingly good at detecting work that you didn't produce.

Students are often shocked that teachers can tell from the style of a paper that it isn't original work, but an experienced professor usually can spot plagiarism across the room. And, in the age of Google, it's very easy to quickly check on the source for almost anything.

What's more, anti-plagiarism software now gives professors powerful tools to use against cheaters.

You've learned effective study strategies from this book and they will help you manage your time and produce good work. This tip is just a reminder to guard against the temptation to buy a term-paper from the internet or cut and paste from others' writing.

Your professors will know it's not your work, and such an impulsive act can be disastrous for your grades—and even your college career.

Tip #21 *Develop backup plans.*

We'll end the "bonus tips" section with a non-academic hint that is nonetheless very important. Develop backup systems for yourself.

You're probably familiar with "Murphy's Law," which says, "Everything that CAN go wrong, WILL go wrong." This seems to be particularly true when you are under stress, or rushing to meet a deadline.

One typical time for things to really go wrong, then, is during the week of final exams.

So, a few minutes spent in planning for bad luck can really pay off.

Think about what is most crucial in your busy days, and *how you'd be impacted if things went wrong.*

What if you lost your car keys? Your house keys?

What if your wallet or purse was stolen with your credit-cards in it? What if your computer dies?

What if your laptop was stolen, or your hard-drive crashes beyond repair?

These, unfortunately, are the kinds of things that happen regularly in daily life. As predicted by Murphy's Law, they seem to happen at the worst possible times, so plan ahead.

Be sure you have an extra car key—maybe in your wallet or briefcase. Give an extra house key to a friend or hide it securely outside (but not under the doormat which is NOT a secure hiding place).

Keep a list in a safe place of the phone numbers to report a lost or stolen credit card so you won't be frantically searching for those numbers if your card is stolen or lost.

If your tires are wearing thin, or your car's battery is old, take remedial action BEFORE you're stranded on a dark and stormy night. Worn tires and old batteries won't heal themselves.

Know where the computer lab is in school in case your hard drive or printer dies, or which of your friends has a computer that you could use.

If you have young children, you know how crucial it is to have backup babysitters and child-care options.

And, for goodness sake, back up important files! The more important they are, the more places they should be backed up. Automatic online backup is often a really good—and easy—thing to do and it can give you great peace of mind about the security of your work.

With some foresight and a little advance planning, you can keep these problems from ruining your day, your week, or the entire semester.

That way, you'll have more time and energy to spend on all the productive and fun things college has to offer.

Chapter 17

Top Tips from Seven Successful College Students

An effective technique taught by "success coaches" is to find people who excel in your field and study what they do.

Since your field right now is going to college, we sought out seven highly successful college students for short interviews. Each took a different road through college, and each had a favorite real-world tips to share.

We picked students who attended many different kinds of colleges, but we only chose students with outstanding grades.

And since graduate school is the next step for most high-achieving college students, we located medical-school, graduate-school, and law-school students whose demanding academic workload has actually increased since college, so these smart-study techniques are *even more* important for them now.

We asked them to describe both their favorite study strategy and something that does not work well for them, or that seems counter-productive.

Here are their answers.

Chris G.

Chris G was a history major at the University of Georgia. He now has an MD degree from the Yale University School of Medicine and is doing advanced research at Harvard.

Q: What study tip do you think works exceptionally well for you?

I always find it very helpful if I *plan for big study events*, for times when I know I have a lot of studying to do.

So, if I am preparing for an exam, for example, I plan *in advance* to spend all morning in the library. It's almost as if once I tell myself that the morning will be devoted to serious study, then I'm programmed to follow through and do nothing else.

It's *the act of telling myself* that a particular block of time WILL be study time that makes it easier for me because that's what I expect to do with that block of time.

If I just sort of wait until I start studying without pre-planning the time, it's likely that it won't happen, or that I'll constantly interrupt myself with other things, whereas if I simply tell myself that "Thursday morning (or whatever) I will spend working on a particular subject," then I'm much, much more likely to follow through.

I see lots of students just fritter away their study time because they didn't set aside time that is ONLY for studying. This has been a really helpful approach for me all through school, and I still use it.

Q: What have you learned doesn't work for you?

I'm a musician, too, and music is very important to me.

But I find that I absolutely can NOT study while listening to music. I find myself getting distracted—and I guess it's because I'm so involved with music that it doesn't stay in the background.

So, if I have music playing while I'm studying, I find that I'm reading the same passage over and over and over, because I'm paying too much attention to the music.

I love music, understand, but I have found that I cannot combine it with serious study.

Katherine K.

Katherine K went to Georgia Tech and majored in Industrial and Systems Engineering.

Q. What study tip do you think works exceptionally well for you?

I would *break assignments down* "as small as possible—down to sections within chapters" and then assign myself times to study each section. I would include break times in my plan so I wouldn't go crazy—sometimes I would actually plan a "walk-around-the-library-break."

And while I studied, I would write down everything I thought was important, and use that for future study. It really helped. I think *I learned a lot more when I took the time to write down what I was studying.* Nobody told me to do this—I just figured it out for myself.

Q. What have you learned doesn't work so well for you?

I could not ever study with a group of people right before a test. If I wasn't really confident of the material, I would psych myself out because I thought that the others knew more than I did, and I would then lose my concentration and focus.

Rob S.

Rob S. has a B. S. in Computer Science from Princeton, and is nearing completion of a Ph.D. in computer science from Carnegie Mellon University.

Q: What study tip do you think works exceptionally well for you?

Location is really important to me when I study, though this is may not be as true for all students.

I like to be in a place that is public, but not too distracting. And I find that I vary where I study depending on what I'm working on, so I might go to a coffee shop for something creative, but to a more solitary spot in the library for something that requires deep concentration.

It's almost a ritual with me to find the right locations for studying and now there are several places that have become my "regular study spots."

Q. What have you learned doesn't work so well for you?

I think I have a tendency to beat myself up when I have a lot to do and don't feel that I'm moving ahead very productively. But that's not helpful at all and just leads to feeling bad.

What works better than feeling guilty about not getting anything done, is to just start doing *something* and stick with it for a while. *I then will find that productivity leads to more productivity* (but unfortunately, the opposite is true, too).

I also always use to-do lists to get tasks "off my brain" so I'm not constantly thinking and worrying about all the things I have yet to do, because worrying is just not helpful.

Laura D.

Laura D. has a B. S. in biology from Harvard and an MD degree from Yale University School of Medicine.

Q: What study tip do you think works exceptionally well for you?

I have found that *I really need it to be quiet* where I study, and that usually means the library. However, even in medical school, I've found that many students go to the library, sit at large tables, and end up spending more time socializing than studying.

I prefer to study really hard when I'm studying, so I don't study at those large tables where my friends congregate.

Instead, I find a small study carrel in the library—actually I usually go to the same one on an upper floor. There is just a small table big enough for me, and it's by a window, which is great. I find that I get much, much more done when I'm working hard, by myself, and in a quiet place without distractions.

Q: What have you learned doesn't work for you?

Well, it's sort of the flip side of my positive answer. I just cannot do serious work when I am surrounded by my friends. It's too distracting. No offense to my friends, of course, but I have to have quiet without distractions if I'm studying hard material. That's just my bottom line.

Laura G.

Laura G. has a B. A. in French from the University of North Carolina at Chapel Hill and is now in an MBA program at Georgia Tech.

Q: What study tip do you think works exceptionally well for you?

I try to *recopy my class notes* the same day, and I find this very helpful in learning the new information.

Sometimes I'm more diligent with this at the beginning of the semester than later, when I am really busy, but it's very helpful to me when I do it. I really make an effort to do this every day, especially in my harder classes.

And my favorite study technique is to write questions on a sheet of paper, and then practice answering them. *I have to write the questions out*—I use notebook paper rather than cards—for this to really work.

Q: What have you learned doesn't work for you?

Studying in groups is often really not effective for me.

I've found that I really prefer to work by myself when possible. But graduate business school requires lots of group projects, and I've found that it's very important to be on a group with people who are serious about getting the work done.

Sometimes you can't control the makeup of the group, but often you choose who to collaborate with, and I've found that is really important because I just don't have any time to waste now that I'm in graduate school.

Elizabeth P.

Elizabeth P. has a B. A. in English from the University of Chicago, graduated from George Washington University Law School, and now practices law in Denver.

Q: What study tip do you think works exceptionally well for you?

I found that if I *approached studying as if it were a job*, then all the looming work seemed less overwhelming.

Especially with the work load in law school, I would go to school at 8 and not leave the library until 6, *just as if it were a job*. I got to where it was more helpful to think about the time spent rather than the number of tasks completed.

In other words, it helped me to *expect* to spend those long days studying, and they fairly quickly became part of my routine daily schedule.

And, I found it very helpful to plan regular breaks, even if I didn't feel burned out—every hour I would get up for 5 or 10 minutes and just walk around. It helped a lot, somehow.

Q: What have you learned doesn't work for you?
Don't get lost in the details. *The big picture can get you a long way*. If you know general principles—about economics, the reasons for WWII, or the motivation behind a work of literature, you can infer a lot.

In law, it's all about IRAC: issue, rule, analysis, and conclusion. If you can *identify* what question you need to answer and know the general rule (or general big-picture situation), all you have to do is apply it to the given facts and summarize your conclusion, but having a clear grasp of the big picture is the key.

I really wish I'd had that kind of concept as an undergrad!

Breen C.
Breen C. is applying to Ph. D. programs in Psychology after graduating from Georgia State University.

Q: What study tip do you think works exceptionally well for you?

I think I'm pretty easily distracted, so I need it to be deathly quiet where I study. So I found that the designated "quiet floor" in the university library was the place that worked for me.

And I can't listen to music or anything else while I'm studying. I might comprehend 90 percent of the reading, but I'll guarantee you that at least 10 percent (and probably more) of my attention is diverted by music. I just can't do it.

I need quiet when I study. It took me a while to figure that out, but once I did, everything became much easier for me.

Q: What have you learned doesn't work for you?

It's interesting to me that I can't shift quickly between subjects when I have a lot to do. I have found that it only works for me to work on ONE subject for a good while. Then I'll take a break before pulling out work for another class. I'll even take a break to watch a TV program or something in between different subjects.

And, honestly, if I have really big projects like I did last semester with three semi-related psych classes, sometimes I would designate days to study just ONE subject. They were so similar that I'd get confused, so it helps me a lot to just do one thing at a time.

I had a pretty rough start to my college life, but *when I realized that no one was making me go to school, I got serious*, I started really studying hard.

I just graduated *magna cum laude*, so I guess it worked!

Chapter 18

Making A's—Onward and Upward

You now have a broad array of specific skills, techniques, methods, hints, tips, and approaches to use as you go through college, graduate school, and on into your work life after graduation.

And you've read top tips from seven high-achieving college students.

All these ideas will work, *and just one of them may be all that's needed to propel you to the top.*

Some of the ideas presented in this book are very simple—*but the key to success is using them, putting the ideas into daily practice.* Reviewing new material each day, for example, isn't a difficult concept to understand but it may be very difficult to actually do.

I've used each of these ideas and strategies with hundreds of college and graduate school students, and I've also taught them to high-school students and even to physicians who were studying for advanced board examinations. All the ideas you've learned are tried, tested, and proven.

They all work, but *none of the study techniques presented here will help you at all if you don't use them.*

So, I really hope you'll see this book as a guidebook for a journey.

As you go through college, you may need to improve different learning skills at different times as you face new challenges. This book will be a useful place to review ideas to improve your reading, studying, test-taking, stress-management, and so on while you are in college.

Through this book, I've suggested simple *Personal Learning System Action Steps*. Though it may seem unnecessary, I hope you'll actually do these steps. When you do, you'll be building *your own Personal Learning System* profile and developing a custom plan for improving your own study style.

And, when active study methods become new habits, you'll see your grades improve. When that happens, you'll be opening more doors for your future.

College is a wonderful and stimulating time for students. Among many other exciting aspects, it gives you a chance to devote yourself to learning new things, and learning is one of the most satisfying parts of life.

Learning is exhilarating, and doing your best is very fulfilling. I firmly believe that the more you learn, the more you'll enjoy life.

Best wishes to you for an exciting, productive, and successful college career.

And always remember: *by the yard it's hard, but by the inch it's a cinch!*

Chapter 19

Eleven Commandments for College Success

1. *Remember WHY good grades in college are important* to your future. Good grades open doors. Poor grades almost certainly close them.

2. *Go to class*. Research proves that class attendance is the best single predictor of college success. And, you're paying a lot of money for tuition. Why waste it?

3. Learn to *manage digital distraction*. If you don't control your digital world, it will steal your time and maybe more.

4. *Organize your time*. Use calendars and to-do lists to get a clear view of assignments and projects so you are in control and not constantly stressed.

5. *Don't fall behind*. Do everything you can to stay current in each class because falling behind doubles your work.

6. *Improve your reading.* Most new knowledge comes through reading, and even a little improvement in speed and comprehension will pay big benefits.

7. *Be active when you study.* If your brain isn't in gear, you're just going through the motions and wasting time.

8. *Find a good place to study.* Maybe it's the library, or maybe it's a coffee shop, but find a place where you can concentrate and not be disturbed.

9. *Study by the question-and-answer method.* This guarantees that you are active when you are spending time studying and is one of the best ways to learn.

10. *Get help if you need it*; it's always available. Find a tutor for help with a specific course, or visit your college's counseling center for personal problems. Use the resources that your college provides.

11. *Be an "extra credit student."* Go further than you need to, read more than the minimum, learn as much as you can, and your college years will be a very successful, enjoyable chapter in your life.

If You Found This Book Helpful, Would You Tell Others?

We truly hope you've found *Making A's in College* helpful in your daily college life. We've tried to fill it with the kinds of practical tips and techniques that have helped so many thousands of other college students.

If you've found this book to be helpful, would you do one quick thing to help other students?

Would you write a short review on Amazon to share your thoughts? *Just a few short words* would make a lot of difference! Sometimes very short reviews are the most helpful .

Just scroll down to the end of the reviews, and click the *Write a Customer Review* box. It's simple and quick.

We, the authors, would truly appreciate it—and so will other college students around the world who will benefit from your review.

Thank you, and again, we hope you've found this book to be helpful—and that your college years (and your life thereafter) will be filled with great success!

About the Authors

Sandra U. Gibson, Ph.D. directed the Learning Assistance Center at Georgia State University in Atlanta for over 25 years, where she worked with thousands of students, conducted popular workshops, and did extensive research in learning.

Her Ph.D. is in reading, and she used that knowledge to develop popular hands-on study skills programs and workshops for college and high-school students. She has also worked with hundreds of individual students to help them learn how to learn more effectively, and her *Making A's in College* video workshop is still widely used in colleges around the world.

James Gibson, M.A. taught high school English and was a writer and photographer for the Georgia Department of Education.

He later taught in, and chaired, the Music Industry program in Georgia State University's School of Music. He has written many newspaper and magazine articles, four books on the music industry, and several children's books. He owns a small record label in Atlanta and writes on a wide variety of subjects.

Points to Remember, Tips to Try

Points to Remember, Tips to Try

Made in the USA
Las Vegas, NV
12 August 2023

75989404R00115